THE THAMES & SEVERN CANAL
HISTORY & GUIDE

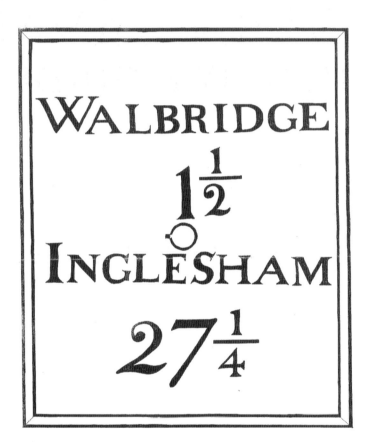

THE THAMES & SEVERN CANAL
HISTORY & GUIDE

DAVID VINER

TEMPUS

For Lin,
towpath companion still

About the Author

David Viner has written extensively on the Thames & Severn Canal and Cotswold social history and has compiled seven albums of historical photographs. This new History & Guide is a worthy successor to his *Stroudwater & Thames and Severn Canals Towpath Guide* (1984 and 1988) written with Michael Handford, which had such a dramatic effect in promoting access to the Cotswold Canals and increasing interest in their history and preservation.

Born in Tetbury in 1947 and educated in Cirencester, with a degree in history from the University of Reading, David Viner was Curator of the Corinium Museum in Cirencester from 1971 to 1998 and Curator of Museums & Arts for Cotswold District Council from 1974-1998.

A writer and lecturer throughout that period, he is now a museums and heritage consultant and a freelance curator and writer, a range of activity which has given him the opportunity to re-visit the Thames & Severn throughout its length and to study afresh a subject which has been an abiding interest and pleasure for over thirty years.

First published 2002
Reprinted 2003

PUBLISHED IN THE UNITED KINGDOM BY:
Tempus Publishing Ltd
The Mill, Brimscombe Port
Stroud, Gloucestershire GL5 2QG

PUBLISHED IN THE UNITED STATES OF AMERICA BY:
Tempus Publishing Inc.
2 Cumberland Street
Charleston, SC 29401

British Library Cataloguing in Publication Data.
A catalogue record for this book is available from the British Library.

ISBN 0 7524 1761 4

Typesetting and origination by Tempus Publishing.
Printed in Great Britain by Midway Colour Print, Wiltshire.

Contents

Acknowledgements

With over thirty years of interest in the Thames & Severn, my indebtedness to a great many people cannot be listed in full here, but it is appropriate to acknowledge such ready assistance with thanks, to local residents and landowners along the route, local historians, collectors of photographic records, colleagues in museums and the fascinating world of industrial archaeology and not least fellow walkers – all of whom have made the preparation of this study a pleasure. My files bulge with kindnesses rendered, too many to list. Not all of those folk are still with us of course, except as happy memories.

Particular thanks are due to the following for helping to make sense of my disparate thoughts: Edwin Cuss of Cirencester, for a happy revival of earlier efforts in canal study; Ron and Doreen Phelps of Cricklade and Brian Gegg of Cirencester for sharing their respective family histories; John Espley of Canalside Miniatures of Wootton Bassett for many useful snippets of information; Ray Wilson of the Gloucestershire Society for Industrial Archaeology (GSIA), especially for help with the research projects of the Society in its early years in the 1960s; and Theo Stening of Tetbury who unearthed information hidden from view for years. The gathering together of a large number of photographs and other illustrations also relies upon the generosity of many people, and all are thanked collectively here. Specific acknowledgement to the original source of each photograph is included with each caption together with copyright details if known. Unless otherwise stated, all illustrations are from the author's own collection. My indebtedness to the kindness over many years of other collectors will be apparent, especially to Howard Beard and Edwin Cuss. Without access to the collections of the late Humphrey Household, the late Frank Lloyd and the late Stan Gardiner, this study would have been much the poorer.

Amongst other thanks, it is a particular pleasure to acknowledge the ready support of past and present colleagues working in those public services which safeguard the historical records upon which any study of this kind relies. Nicholas Kingsley and his staff at the Gloucestershire Record Office shoulder the great burden (and wonderful opportunity) of the extensive Thames & Severn archive, surely one of the jewels in its not-inconsiderable crown; David McDougall at the National Waterways Museum in Gloucester was more helpful and generous than I could hope for and once again made free with his knowledge of the canal network; also in Llanthony Warehouse, Roy Jamieson kindly gave me access to the British Waterways archives. Judy Mills and Lisa Gaunt in the Corinium Museum, Cirencester, and Nigel Cox in the Gloucester Folk Museum were as helpful and supportive as ever, and special thanks are due to Hugh Morrison at the Museum in the Park at Stroud, who gave ready access for study to the collections in his care, and not least to his extensive knowledge of the Frome valley and its history. As I have good reason to know, the museum and archive services provided by the various authorities in Gloucestershire rely a great deal upon the skills and knowledge of staff members such as these.

Bruce Hall, Chairman of the Cotswold Canals Trust since 1988, and his council members and staff over the years have welcomed my attempts to look back, when they themselves were preoccupied with looking forward. Bruce, Ken Burgin, Keith Harding and Maureen Poulton

Chalford wharf on 29 April 1937. Maintenance is underway on the roundhouse. The canal, closed four years before, stands idle. (Photo courtesy Humphrey Household)

were especially helpful on several occasions (and at short notice) and my debt to current editor David Jowett and previous editors of *The Trow* will be obvious throughout these pages. Richard Fairhurst kindly made available the map on page 17. Hugh Conway-Jones gave me useful information on several occasions at just the right moment, and his own new study *The Gloucester & Sharpness Canal – An Illustrated History* is due out in 2003. At the same time, Joan Tucker's new study *The Stroudwater Navigation – A Social History* is also planned to appear, thus providing enthusiasts and local historians with a rich feast of Gloucestershire canal material. It is appropriate, therefore, to acknowledge the contribution to canal historical studies which Tempus Publishing of Brimscombe (appropriately housed in Port Mill alongside Brimscombe Port) are making by publishing all three volumes; in a very real sense Tempus is taking over the task so comprehensively advanced by David & Charles and later developed by Alan Sutton Publishing from the 1960s onwards. For the company Campbell McCutcheon is to be particularly thanked for his commitment to this aim as well as for his supportive approach throughout to the task in hand. In guiding and developing this catalogue my good friend Alan Sutton of Tempus Publishing continues to oversee and ensure a significant and permanent contribution to historical studies in his – and my – home county of Gloucestershire.

My final and greatest acknowledgement is to my wife Linda. This project, like all our other projects, is very much a shared activity and she has undertaken much of the background research for this study. By rights this volume should also have joint authorship, but modesty dictates otherwise. To dedicate this volume in thanks to her for the continued companionship along this particular towpath is but a token of a greater acknowledgement along the longer towpath of life.

David Viner
Cirencester
August 2002

Extracts from 'The Book of Rules'

The 'The Book of Rules' was issued to all employees of the Canal Company, to the boatmen and to all others who used the canal.

Rules Orders and Regulations
To be observed by
Bargemen, Watermen, Boatmen
And other persons
Using the
Thames and Severn Canal Navigation

The Acts of Parliament, (23 George III, c.38, and George III, c.181) declare:

That any Person who shall wilfully or maliciously damage the works of this Canal, shall be deemed guilty of Felony, and be punishable by Transportation, or otherwise, as the Court shall adjudge.

That any Person who shall wantonly, or carelessly, open any Lock, Paddle, Valve, or Clough, or shall suffer any Vessel to run against or strike upon any Locks or Bridges, or shall draw of the Water, or leave any Clough open and running after any vessel shall have passed any Lock or shall open any Paddle, Valve, or Clough, in the Lock gates, so as to waste or mis-spend the water, shall forfeit for every such offence, a sum not exceeding Five Pounds, nor less than Twenty Shillings.

That the Owner or Master of every Vessel shall be made answerable for any damage done by his Vessel, or the men belonging to or employed in the same, to the Works of the Canal, or by loading or unloading, or for any damage or trespass committed on the Owners of adjoining Lands and buildings.

That the name of the Master of every Vessel must be painted on each side thereof in large capital letters. Any Vessel may be measured at the will of the Company. Any Master neglecting to put his name on a vessel, or afterwards defacing it or destroying the Gauge Marks, or refusing to have his Vessel measured, or to produce his certificate of the Gauge, shall, for any one of these offences, forfeit Forty Shillings.

That any Person bathing in the Canal, without permission, subjects himself to a penalty of Forty Shillings for every offence; and in default of payment, imprisonment and hard labour for one month.

That any Person who shall throw Ballast, Gravel, Stones, or Rubbish into the Canal, shall forfeit a sum not exceeding Ten Pounds.

Introduction

Any study of the Thames & Severn Canal begins with at least two great advantages. Firstly, there is access to what the distinguished canal historian Charles Hadfield called 'probably the finest set of individual canal archives in the country' now preserved in the Gloucestershire Record Office, and secondly there are the fruits of detailed and meticulous research over many years on those same archives (plans, notes, company reports and minutes etc.) by Humphrey Household, the principal historian of the canal, whose study *The Thames & Severn Canal* (David & Charles 1969 with a new edition by Alan Sutton Publishing in 1983) is still widely regarded as one of the best single studies of any canal on the British canal network. In addition, an even greater body of information is contained within the same author's thesis for the University of Bristol, completed in 1958 (see Further Reading). For detailed reference to particular aspects of the story, one can do no better than return to these original sources and the presentation of them in Household's work.

This present study is but a mere reflection of that considerable achievement. Here, it is possible only to summarise some aspects of the written evidence as an introduction and guide to the study and enjoyment of the Thames & Severn as it now survives on the ground (at July 2002).

Use is made of contemporary record, both in the eye of the bystander or visitor or in the more formal construction and management records of those who worked to keep the project alive and well throughout its life. There is a consistent emphasis upon the industrial archaeology and heritage assets which can still be seen. Although restoration plans are very much in the public eye, it will be obvious that the line largely remains derelict and that the heyday of the canal was well over a century ago, more accurately over 150 years ago. In the period since abandonment of most of the line in 1927 and the remainder at the western end in 1933, so much has happened which relegated the canal to be an increasingly distant (but not forgotten) aspect of commercial and transport history in the Cotswolds, rotting away largely out of sight.

Its former significance as part of a national communications network suggests that it might have deserved a better fate than oblivion, and indeed the restoration campaign launched exactly thirty years ago by the Cotswold Canals Trust (and its predecessor bodies the Stroudwater Canal Society and from 1975 the Stroudwater, Thames & Severn Canal Trust) has steadily built up support and political will, linked with a regular programme of action on the ground, so that the 'why?' and 'what for?' questions of the early 1970s have largely been replaced by 'how?' and 'when?'. As with all areas of expenditure in the public domain, the accompanying question of 'how much?' remains a common factor and an important issue. Even so, new forms of predominantly leisure use for such a considerable heritage asset are now in prospect.

Growing up in Cirencester, I was aware of the town's canal wharf as little more than a relic, being utilised as the municipal depot. Within a few years during the early 1960s, it was joined in its demise by the town's railway network (Cirencester boasted two stations and two quite separate lines) as the surviving remains of both canal and railway suffered considerable reduction as a result of the creation of a new inner ring road for the town during the 1970s. As one of Cirencester's many young archaeologists during those heady days of re-shaping the town, I well remember discovering by chance in 1969 the culverted leat which supplied water into the canal wharf. We were looking for things Roman, and this story of eighteenth-century commercial development did not have high priority. However, my rather tentative enquiry about it to canal historian Charles Hadfield, who lived nearby in South Cerney, brought forth an encouraging response and a personal recommendation to Humphrey Household, whose long-awaited and definitive study of the Thames & Severn Canal was about to be published a few months later. Quite by chance, another if smaller study, the charming booklet by John Espley and W.E. Duncan Young appeared only three weeks before Household's own work.

I little appreciated then how formative these contacts were to become. From then on, a steady (and treasured) correspondence with Household and others opened my eyes to the fascinating story of this canal, and fortune smiled upon the publication of a photographic album in 1975 which was well received and helped generate public interest. By this time the restoration campaign had begun in earnest, and the thoroughly enjoyable research for and publication of the *Stroudwater & Thames and Severn Canals Towpath Guide* in 1984 (reprinted in 1988) brought a whole new group of interested people into range. Some thirty years of study and enjoyment of the canal and its industrial archaeology have introduced me to a wide range of often committed supporters of canal history and restoration (as well as opponents too of course) and this enjoyable process continues. The present study is offered as but the latest instalment in a continuing saga.

In 1985 Michael Handford (who wrote the Stroudwater sections of the *Towpath Guide*) and I looked forward to our work being quickly out of date as the pace of restoration and re-investment gathered pace. How right we were! In revisiting that text for the present publication, the steady progress made in winning hearts and minds, and indeed money, is remarkable and should stand as an exemplar to other heritage amenity projects, where the apparent impossibility of the task can be whittled down incrementally in the context of a long-term vision.

The following pages reveal something of those changes, set into the broader picture of a canal which had a beginning, a middle (or perhaps several) and a long and slow ending. These can be chronicled into the late eighteenth century, throughout the nineteenth century and steadily into the early decades of the twentieth century. Surviving photographic evidence is not of course balanced throughout these stages of life and death, and pictures of the canal at work remain rare indeed. However, there is a good body of material from the early twentieth century, and then as the deterioration increased the romanticism which often goes with that also increased, so that the twentieth century history of the Thames & Severn can now be quite well documented photographically. An attempt has been made here to show evidence of that valuable archive, and to acknowledge the public and amenity bodies, as well as private sources, which now care for much of it on behalf of the community at large.

Revisiting the 1984 text and walking the line yet again, I was reminded how many changes have occurred even in the twenty years or so since that study was made. Considerable lengths of towpath have been brought back into public access (eastwards from Siddington to Latton

Winter snow adds to the gothic mystery of the western (Daneway) portal of the Sapperton Tunnel, from a photograph taken on 23 February 1947. (Photo courtesy Humphrey Household)

is striking in this regard), sections of canal and their locks look in better condition than they have for decades (again have a look at Siddington), and important structures such as the Daneway portal of the tunnel have been restored. Puck Mill has been rescued from its general dereliction and the wharfhouse at Kempsford restored from its gentle decay. Interestingly, the outside world has intruded in many ways as the particular attractions of roundhouses and isolated buildings as homes have stimulated their increased market value. In recent years the roundhouses at Chalford, Cerney Wick and most recently Inglesham have all been sold, Chalford more than once, and so too the once-derelict wharf cottage at Daneway and its counterpart on the North Wilts junction at Latton Basin. Private as well as public funding is rejuvenating these old buildings and structures, and a balance will always need to be struck to ensure access (visual if not physical) to the community heritage which all this represents.

With the involvement of British Waterways now a reality in the Cotswold Canals restoration project as a key part of a national restoration programme, and with significant funding in prospect, that first part of the restoration story in the thirty years since 1972 may be regarded as largely complete and a whole new challenge awaits. It remains to be seen how the present text will withstand the changes of the next decade or so! Reading through the files, various campaigns since 1970 have offered a range of optimistic predictions for re-opening the canals – the year 2000 being an easy target to select – but that target and others have now come and gone. Meanwhile, forward planning continues in depth, and the beginning of the twenty-first century seems a good time to predict afresh.

Landscaping at Chalford Wharf, with part of the sluice gear from Sevill's Mill re-used in a circular feature mirroring the roundhouse behind. (Photo Robert Carr, Dursley, courtesy Cotswold Canals Trust)

It is also a good time to make a fresh analysis (as well as a record) of changes on the ground. This History & Guide follows other publications on the Thames & Severn by moving – at least as far as the towpath guide is concerned – from west to east, from the Severn (or more correctly the junction with the Stroudwater Canal in Stroud) eastwards to the Thames at Lechlade. West to east remains popular with walkers, and there is some historical validity to this approach, in that the thinking behind the canal route and indeed much of its construction was developed in this way. Equally well, however, an east to west option can be adopted. The route is described as it was finally checked for this book, as at July 2002, and it is a pleasure to record that even at the height of summer the towpath was a joy to walk and explore – some fifteen miles in total where it is properly open and accessible. This excludes the walk over the tunnel and interestingly now divides in terms of mileage almost equally to west and east, a considerable balancing up from earlier years.

Key Access Points are suggested in the text but users of this History & Guide are strongly recommended to acquire the latest OS Explorer maps 168, 169 and 170 as a further source of information on public rights of way etc. Visitor Information Centres, particularly those in Cirencester (Corn Hall, Market Place) and in Stroud (Subscription Rooms in George Street) can provide details of accommodation, pubs and places to eat as well as bus and rail timetables. The Thames & Severn has a good choice of canal-side pubs which are mentioned in the text. To begin a tour of any part of the Thames & Severn (especially the western section), by using the rail stations at Stroud or Kemble on the Gloucester to Swindon line, is to be reminded not only of the considerable beauty of these western Cotswold valleys but also of the rival transport network which featured so largely in the decline and eventual demise of the Thames & Severn itself as a commercial undertaking.

Some issues of spelling crop up in the text. Wallbridge is the place name in Stroud, but in the Canal Company's records both Wallbridge and Walbridge are used, although the latter is consistently preferred for its network of mileplates. Lengthman is interchangeable with watchman (and the Company preferred the latter), and wharfhouse is rendered as a single word as indeed these fascinating buildings were themselves single, integrated units, both homes and storage facilities. No attempt has been made to render any measurements in metric format; the imperial system is preferred as it confirms to the original historical record. For the record, references in this study to 'the Trust' in terms of the restoration campaign of the past thirty years, cover the work of the present Cotswold Canals Trust and all its predecessor bodies. In this connection, the views expressed in this study are those of the author alone, and cannot be taken to represent any other body.

Finally, it should be noted that sections of the towpath and canal bed, and certainly most of the associated land, remain private (as distinct from publicly-owned) property and this privacy should be respected. The mention of any building or structure in this guide does not necessarily confer any rights of access, and users are also advised to exercise extreme care when examining canal structures. Some locks are overgrown, unguarded and deep, and all access is undertaken at the personal risk of the individual, for which no responsibility can be accepted by the writer or publishers of this guide.

However, with care and consideration, visiting and interpreting the remains of the Thames & Severn Canal can be a most rewarding and stimulating experience and is much to be recommended!

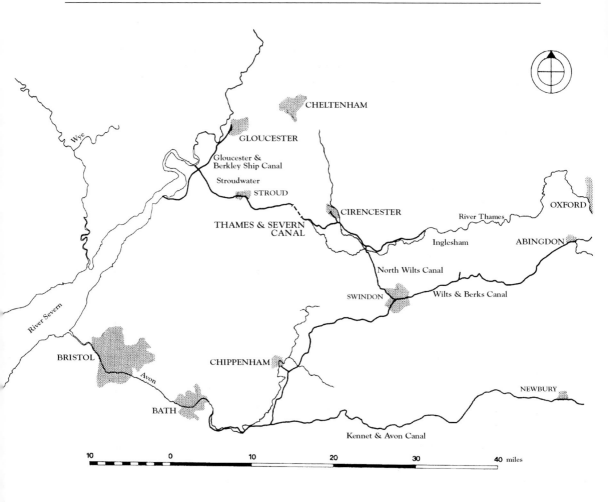

Thames & Severn Canal: Table of Locks

The Stroudwater Navigation
Rises from low water in the River Severn, which is 14ft 5in above ordnance datum, to Walbridge Basin, Stroud, 107ft 2in, in thirteen locks.

The Thames & Seven Canal
In twenty-eight locks rises 241ft from Walbridge to the summit, 348ft 1in above low water, River Severn, and 362ft 6in above ordnance datum. Descends 129ft from the summit to the Thames by sixteen locks, a total of forty-four locks.

	Distance from Walbridge		Rise as recorded in 1810	
	Miles	**Chains**	**Feet**	**Inches**
Locks 68 to 69ft long, 16ft 1in or 16ft 2in wide.				
Wallbridge Lower	0	0	9	0
Wallbridge Upper	0	11	11	0
Bowbridge	0	71	10	0
Griffin's	1	22	10	0
Ham Mill	1	50	9	0 a
Ridler's or Hope Mill	2	1	8	0
Gough's Orchard or Dallaway's or				
Lewis's	2	20	8	0
Lock 90ft long and 16ft 1in wide				
Bourn or Harris's	2	61	11	0
Locks 90 to 93ft long, and 12ft 9in or 13ft wide				
Beale's	3	21	8	0
St Mary's or Clark's	3	52	8	0
Grist Mill or Iles's Mill or				
Wallbank's	3	60	8	0
Ballinger's	3	70	8	0
Chalford Chapel	4	2	8	0
Bell	4	25	10	0
Innell's or Clowes's or Red Lion	4	40	8	0
Golden Valley	4	62	8	0
Baker's Mill or Twizzel's Mill Lower				
later Bolting	5	36	8	0
Baker's Mill or Twizzel's Mill Upper				
or just Baker's Mill	5	44	8	0
Puck Mill Lower	5	64	8	0
Puck Mill Upper	5	70	8	0
Whitehall Lower	6	10	8	0
Whitehall Upper	6	50	8	0 b
Bathurst's Meadow or				
Bathurst's Meadow Lower	6	60	8	0 b
Bathurst's Meadow Upper or				
Sickeridge Wood Lower	6	67	8	0 b
Sickeridge Wood Middle	6	72	8	0 b
Sickeridge Wood Upper	7	0	9	0 b
Daneway Basin or Daneway Lower	7	5	9	0 b
Daneway Bridge or Daneway Upper	7	10	9	0 b

Summit level			*Fall as recorded in 1810*	
	Miles	**Chains**	**Feet**	**Inches**
Siddington Upper	15	23	9	9
Siddington Second	15	26	9	9
Siddington Third	15	30	9	9
Siddington Fourth or Lowest	15	35	9	9
South Cerney Upper	16	60	9	4 c
South Cerney Middle	16	65	9	4 c
South Cerney Lowest	16	73	9	4 c
Boxwell Spring or Shallow or Little Lock	17	45	3	6
Wilmoreway or Wildmoorway Upper or Humpback	18	1	7	6 d
Wilmoreway Lower or just Wilmoreway	18	36	11	0 d
Cerney Wick	19	21	6	0
Latton	20	61	9	4
Eisey	22	40	7	0
Dudgrove Double Lock	28	0		
upper chamber	9	0		
lower chamber	2	6		
Inglesham	28	60	6	2

The distances are as recorded in the Company's Fact Book.

a. Recorded in 1894, almost certainly inaccurately, as 8ft.

b. Rise as recorded in the latter part of the nineteenth century was 8ft 5in.

c. Recorded in 1894, almost certainly inaccurately, as 9ft 3in.

d. Fall as recorded in the latter part of the nineteenth century was 9ft 3in.

When standardised, a chain was a measure of 22 yards (3ft = 1 yard); and a mile was a measure of 1,760 yards (5,280 feet).

[Source : Household *The Thames & Severn Canal* (1983, Appendix 1)]

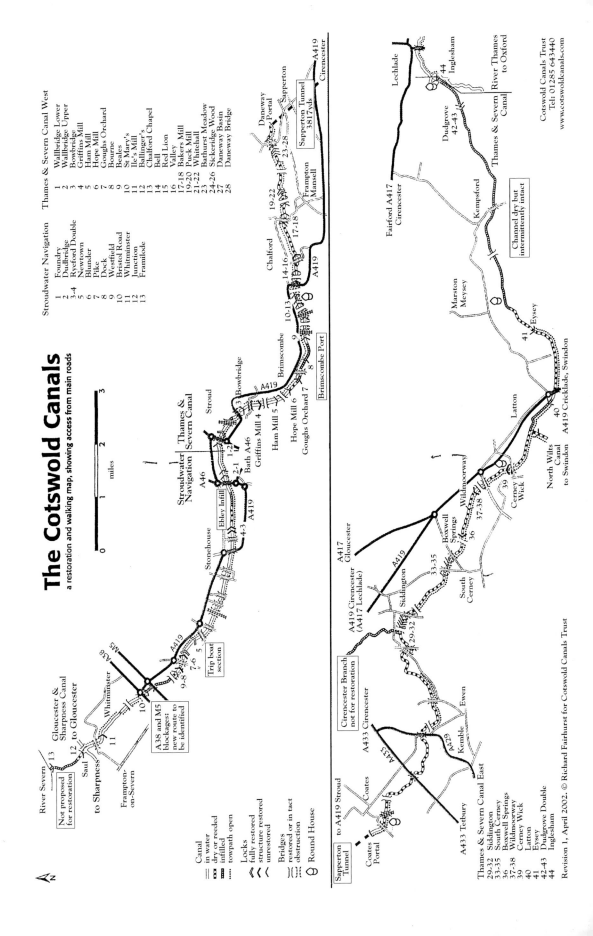

The Cotswold Canals

a restoration and walking map, showing access from main roads

N

miles
0 1 2 3

Thames & Severn Canal West

1 Wallbridge Lower
2 Wallbridge Upper
3 Bowbridge
4 Griffins Mill
5 Ham Mill
6 Hope Mill
7 Goughs Orchard
8 Bourne
9 Beales
10 St Mary's
11 Ile's Mill
12 Ballinger's
13 Chalford Chapel
14 Bell
15 Red Lion
16 Valley
17-18 Bakers Mill
19-20 Puck Mill
21-22 Whitehall
23 Bathurst Meadow
24-26 Sickeridge Wood
27 Daneway Basin
28 Daneway Bridge

Stroudwater Navigation

1 Foundry
2 Dudbridge
3-4 Ryeford Double
5 Newtown
6 Blunder
7 Pike
8 Dock
9 Westfield
10 Bristol Road
11 Whitminster
12 Junction
13 Framilode

Sapperton Tunnel 3817yds

Brimscombe Port

Stroudwater Navigation

Thames & Severn Canal

Ebley Infill

Trip boat section

River Severn

Gloucester & Sharpness Canal
to Gloucester

Not proposed for restoration

to Sharpness

Frampton-on-Severn

Saul

A38 and M5 blockages; new route to be identified

Stonehouse

Stroud

Bowbridge

Brimscombe

Chalford

Daneway Portal

Sapperton

Frampton Mansell

Cirencester Branch not for restoration

Coates Portal

Tetbury

Coates

Kemble

Ewen

Siddington

South Cerney

Boxwell Springs

Wildmoorway

Cerney Wick

North Wilts Canal to Swindon

Cricklade, Swindon

Latton

Eysey

Marston Meysey

Kempsford

Dudgrove

Inglesham

Lechlade

River Thames to Oxford

Fairford

Channel dry but intermittently intact

Cotswold Canals Trust
Tel: 01285 643440
www.cotswoldcanals.com

Thames & Severn Canal East

29-32 Siddington
33-35 South Cerney
36 Boxwell Springs
37-38 Wildmoorway
39 Latton
40 Eysey
42-43 Dudgrove Double
44 Inglesham

Canal
— in water
— dry or reeded
— infilled
···· towpath open

Locks
‹‹‹ fully restored
structure restored
unrestored

Bridges
restored or in tact
obstruction
○ Round House

Revision 1, April 2002. © Richard Fairhurst for Cotswold Canals Trust

1 Historical Summary

In eloquent tones the principal national newspaper, *The Times*, the influential *Gentleman's Magazine* and the local *Gloucester Journal* all recorded the opening of the Thames & Severn Canal in November 1789. Each used much the same source, if not a single source, which effectively captured much of the contemporary wonder at the achievement. Even allowing for the exuberance of the language, considerable insight can be gained into the impact of this new canal by studying the words of contemporaries.

Gloucester Journal for 30 November 1789

> *On Thursday last was effected the greatest object of internal navigation in this kingdom. The Severn was united to the Thames by an intermediate Canal, ascending by Stroud, through the Vale of Chalford, to the height of [347] feet by 40 locks; there entering a tunnel through the hill of Saperton, for the length of two miles and three furlongs, and descending by 22 locks it joined the Thames near Lechlade.*
>
> *A boat, with an union flag on her mast-head, passed laden for the first time to St John's Bridge, below Lechlade, in the presence of great numbers of people who were assembled on the occasion; and who answered a salute of twelve pieces of cannon from Buscot Park by loud huzzas. A dinner was given at five of the principal inns at Lechlade, and the day ended with ringing of bells, a bonfire and a ball. With respect to the internal commerce of the kingdom, and the security of communication in time of war, this junction of the Thames and Severn must be attended with the most beneficial consequences. Among other advantages, stone for building, with which the hills near Bisley abound, and for paving in the Forest of Dean, may now reach London at an easy rate. All the heavy articles from the mines and foundries in the heart of Wales, and the counties contiguous to the Severn, may find a secure and certain conveyance to the capital.*
>
> *In short, this undertaking is worthy of a great commercial nation, and does credit to the exertions of the individuals, who have promoted and completed a work of such magnitude, at an expence of near £200,000.*
>
> *The arched tunnel carried through the bowels of a mountain, near two miles and half long, and fifteen wide, at a level 250ft below its summit, is a work worthy of admiration and the locks leading from Stroud are executed in a manner deserving commendation.*

The idea to link the two great rivers of southern Britain was certainly not a new concept. For nearly two centuries before its actual achievement, local and national figures had been making suggestions and recommendations to create a link. Their motivations varied, but all saw the potential benefits to trade in providing as direct an access as possible for sources of supply and manufacture to the capital city on the Thames.

Before the eighteenth century, when the line actually adopted through the Frome valley and Stroud came to be chosen, proposals were advanced from time to time for other lines of connection between the Severn and Thames. Their study on the ground would also be a fascinating exercise, not least because several would have crossed areas of undoubted natural beauty not easily associated to the modern eye with canal construction. Indeed the adopted route was only just successful over an alternative line from Tewkesbury and Cheltenham, linking with the River Coln through Bibury and Fairford and thence to the Thames at Lechlade. Other routes also had their supporters and this searching for a successful line gives an indication of the enormity of the task of cutting through the Cotswold scarp at a suitable point.

The construction of Sapperton Tunnel was regarded at the time, and has been ever since, as one of the engineering achievements of the day. It took five and a half years to build and extended over two and a quarter miles through the Cotswold hills. Its construction was riven with difficulties but the final achievement is symbolic not only of the energy and enthusiasm of eighteenth century canal 'developers' but also of the construction gangs who risked life and limb (and occasionally lost both) to cut the line through. In fact, the actual period of construction of the Thames & Severn (virtually thirty miles in total length) was a mere six years and seven months, from the passing of the Act of authorisation on 17 April 1783. This compares well with progress on the ground made by other contemporary schemes and we must realise, of course, that many such schemes were themselves deadly rivals for the shortest and the quickest route between two centres. Hence the completion of the Thames & Severn late in 1789 came only a few weeks before the long-awaited completion of the Oxford Canal into Oxford in January 1790 and the junction between the Coventry and the Birmingham Canals in July that same year. All three were effectively competing for the route to London

Donkey and boat at Coatesfield on the summit level of the Thames & Severn Canal at Coates, one of the few illustrations of working boats on the canal in the nineteenth century.

for West Midlands goods and resources, and each was spurred on by the progress of its rival. In this aspect of the history of canals, the men who cut the Thames & Severn – and the promoters who financed the project – made a good account of themselves.

A meeting held in Cirencester in September 1781 to promote the idea of the canal proved to be the turning point; those involved deciding very quickly to seek professional advice and in doing so they turned to a man who was probably the most outstanding canal engineer of the day, Robert Whitworth. He had been a pupil of James Brindley, the great canal builder, and had developed his skills in draughtsmanship and site survey for various promoters of intended lines of canals, together with his actual experience in canal engineering.

In fact when Whitworth was called in the Thames & Severn promoters were still divided on the best line for the canal and this and other reasons may have lain behind the rather nebulous instructions given to him in carrying out his survey. He was, for example, given no guidelines on the scale of the cut, and this was a particularly difficult problem in view of the three different sizes of vessels which were to be expected to use the through route when complete: the 15ft width of the Severn trows, the 12ft width of the western barges of the Thames and the narrower 7ft variety of canal boat which later became ubiquitous on the canal system as long boats or 'narrow boats'. In fact, Whitworth assumed that the dimensions required related to the Thames barge and that transhipment at one point would be necessary. His assumption was that the vessels of the Thames could navigate the gauges applicable to the Severn, whereas the reverse was not possible.

Whitworth visited Cirencester in December 1781 when the proprietors commissioned him to begin his survey which was, however, not forthcoming for a further year as the result of commitments elsewhere. He made a further assumption of some significance, in that an exact and thorough survey was not required of him. As a result he set out 'to form a proper judgement of the surveys already made' and to compare the practicability and expense of the alternative routes then under discussion. He found that the 'Cirencester line' – that is the line eventually selected and built – had a number of advantages; it would require a lower summit (hence less lockage) and it would have a total length of seven and a half miles less than the Tewkesbury-Cheltenham-Lechlade line. It was also noted that the water yield from the Churn and the Frome would far exceed that of the springs in the upper Coln Valley, leaving aside the additional difficulties of the latter route in gaining access to water and problems with supplies to mills on the river. His estimate for the Cirencester line was £127,916 4s 0d for a total of twenty-nine miles and three and a half furlongs.

The major problem noted in the report was a section where the line of the summit level ran through 'some very bad rocky ground, which cannot be avoided for several miles altogether, that is worse than I have ever seen any canal cut through for such a continued length'. This proved to be a well-justified warning as subsequent efforts to retain an adequate supply of water in the summit level were to prove. Despite such difficulties and the distinct lack of measurement in detail for cutting the line (reservoirs, wharves, warehouses and water compensation costs were all excluded from the estimate), the promoters adopted this route in January 1783. Three months later came the passing of the Act [23 Geo III Cap. 38] and within weeks James Perry, the company's first superintendent, had nearly 200 men at work along the line. As an example from the records, on 10 June 1783 Charles Kinner, described as a 'navvy', was paid four shillings for 'Taking up a hedge'. From then on, the story is largely

RATES OF TONNAGE ON THE THAMES & SEVERN CANAL NAVIGATION.

Coal or Coke	Entering the Canal at Walbridge, and landed short of, or at the Wharf of the Thames and Severn Canal at Stroud, per Ton. From Walbridge, delivered at any place above the Stroud Wharf, or in the Basin at Brimscombe Port, 1s. per Ton. From Walbridge, passing the Bourne Lock, and delivered at Cirencester, or any intermediate place, 1s. 3d. per Ton. From Walbridge Vessels passing Siddington Locks will be charged 2s. 6d. per Ton, and reduced by drawback to any place between Siddington and Latton or Cricklade Wharf, to 1s. 8d. per Ton. From Walbridge Vessels landing their Cargoes at Buscot on the River Thames, or short of Ensham, reduced by drawback to 2s. per Ton. From Walbridge Vessels taking their Cargoes into the North Wilts Canal, or below Ensham on the River Thames, reduced by drawback to 1s. per Ton.
Timber, &c.	The Act of Parliament requiring Round Oak, Ash, or Elm Timber, to be computed at 50 cubic feet, and Square of the same kinds at 40 feet; Fir or Deal Balk, Poplar, Beech, or Birch, Round or Square, at 50 feet cube to the Ton. A Tonnage of 1½d. per Ton per Mile will be charged between Walbridge and any place on the Canal, or short of Ensham, on the River Thames; and in like manner the same rate of 1½d. per Ton per Mile will be charged on all Cargoes coming Westward, subject to the Regulation as below. Timber, Deals, or Building Materials, going the whole length of the Canal, and delivered below Ensham on the River Thames, will be reduced by drawback to 1s. per Ton for the whole distance.
Grain of all kinds	Passing along the Canal, Westward, will be chargeable with the reduced rate of one Half-penny per Ton per Mile, subject to the Conditions below, except that coming from the North Wilts Canal. Any of the Company's Warehouses will be open to receive Grain waiting for Vessels free of any charge, and may remain during the pleasure of the Sender, provided there is room in the Warehouse.
Stone	From any of the Quarries on the summit level, for the repair of the Wilts and Berks Canal, or delivered at or beyond Cricklade Wharf, or taken into the North Wilts Canal, or passing along the Thames and Severn Canal Westward; the charge for the whole distance will be 6d. per Ton.
Goods or Merchandise	Of all kinds whatsoever, not before enumerated, passing along the Canal, Eastward or Westward, will be charged at the rate of 1d. per Ton per Mile.
N. Wilts or Wilts & Berks Canal. *Charge to or from.*	All Vessels passing along the Thames and Severn Canal, and taking their Cargo into the North Wilts Canal, containing whatsoever they may (Coals included) will be chargeable with the sum of 1s. per Ton for the whole distance (Stone as excepted above).

STROUDWATER CANAL.

	The length of the Stroudwater Navigation is Eight Miles. This Canal connects the Thames and Severn Canal with the River Severn and the Gloucester and Berkeley Canal, and the Rates of Tonnage chargeable on that Navigation on Vessels entering the Thames and Severn Canal are as follows :—
Coal or Coke.....	Delivered at Walbridge or Stroud Wharf, per Ton. Delivered between Stroud Wharf and the Tunnel, per Ton. Delivered beyond the Tunnel, 6d. per Ton. Delivered in the North Wilts or Wilts and Berks Canal, 6d. per Ton.
Stone	Stone, 4d. per Ton.
Goods or Merchandise of all kinds	Goods, per Ton. On all Goods brought from any place beyond the Eastern end of the Thames and Severn Canal Tunnel in Vessels whose preceding Cargo on their up Voyage passed through the Stroudwater Navigation, and which shall be delivered at or beyond the Junction of the Gloucester and Berkeley Canal, 6d. per Ton.

Charges for conveyance of goods along the Thames & Severn and Stroudwater Canals. Undated but early twentieth century. (Courtesy Howard Beard)

an account of the steady progress in construction working east from Stroud, together with the associated task of winning over the landowners along the line to ensure that work could proceed. The construction of the tunnel at Sapperton proved to be an even more hazardous and difficult enterprise than the promoters had imagined.

Among the most significant figures in this early construction period were Josiah Clowes, appointed to be the company's 'surveyor and engineer and head carpenter' at a salary of £300pa, and Samuel Smith, clerk of works, and his assistant Richard Hall whose journal of memoranda from 1784-1794 records something of the day-to-day problems and frustrations in building the canal. The detail of this period of activity is indeed fascinating, and remains well preserved in the manuscript archives in the Gloucestershire Record Office. It seems clear that the proprietors of the Canal Company had hoped that Robert Whitworth would play a larger role in the period of construction. In fact, apart from the initial survey (for which his fee was eighteen guineas) he did little other than mark out the line of the nine-mile-long summit level which included, of course, Sapperton Tunnel. This task alone took up fifty-six days for which he was paid £93 7s 6d.

It fell to Clowes to relate the feasibility scheme to the actual cut of the canal, and alterations and amendments which he made subsequently became a matter of controversy with the canal proprietors when mistakes appeared. The main example of this is the error in levels on either side of the summit, which can be seen to particular advantage in the close proximity of the locks climbing up to Daneway and the inadequate pounds between them. In addition,

Looking down to Daneway from Sapperton village, showing the canal watchman's cottage by the tunnel entrance. (From an original photograph by W. Dennis Moss of Cirencester)

Clowes bore the brunt of the many difficulties resulting from the selection of the hopelessly inadequate contractor Charles Jones to construct the Sapperton Tunnel, and these problems contributed to the length of time it finally took to complete the tunnel.

The actual work of construction proceeded by a system described by Household as 'gang-piecework' under which gang leaders entered into agreements for each task undertaken. From this naturally developed the idea of contractors, men of sufficient experience, bearing or influence to undertake an agreed section of work for a fixed sum. It would be fascinating to know more about such men, nearly all of whom were self-made. On the Thames & Severn, it is possible to see from the records who was employed where and at what cost, and thus to build up a picture of the progress of the works and some of the individuals involved. A number, such as Thomas Cook and John Nock, both stonemasons, became contractors of some stature employing numbers of men. Equally, both were typical of such men travelling from one canal project to another and from one site contract to another, and indeed undertaking various contracts simultaneously. Cook had gained experience on the Stroudwater construction, and Nock on the Stourbridge Navigation. Cook's work on the Thames & Severn covered the period 1784-1795 and included the building of the Brimscombe Port house, and (we may suspect) the Coates portal of the Sapperton Tunnel. During this same period he was the main contractor for the rebuilding of Gloucester Jail between 1786-1791.

Many of the labourers' references are to 'day-works' – a still familiar term – and often indicate the nature of the work undertaken; thus Simon Hamer received £39 17s 7½d. on 14 July 1784 for 'day work and walling at Mr Griffin' i.e. Griffin's Lock. A year later he was working regularly up at Daneway as the cutting approached the summit level. Other outside contractors are also mentioned, for example John Wood, 'carrier at or near Cirencester' received £6 16s 0d. on 7 August 1786 for carrying 13,600 bricks from Siddington (brick yard) to the new feeder being constructed at Cirencester. A year's worth of mole catching along the canal line earned Richard Musto the sum of four guineas in March 1795.

Thus the canal was built and subsequently maintained. There were numerous errors and examples of poor workmanship; some bridges fell down and had to be rebuilt, and later corrections were necessary to faults not appreciated at the time of construction. The shortage of water was always an issue; Boxwell Spring lock was constructed in 1792 to gain access to additional water supplies from nearby springs. Throughout its working life, such tasks of repair and maintenance formed a considerable problem for the proprietors of the Thames & Severn.

The first boat through the entire length of the canal and into the Thames passed through Inglesham lock on 19 November 1789. There followed a century of commercial activity on the Thames & Severn, which merits a full and detailed study in itself. Household summarises this admirably, and includes an account of the dividends paid to shareholders from 1810 through to 1864 – a fairly consistent pattern until a distinct reduction in payments after the mid-1850s and no dividends paid at all after 1864. The pattern is, in fact, a more or less consistent downward trend thereafter, with the continuing problems of maintenance, tackled with such determination at intervals during the first half of the nineteenth century, continuing to drain resources from then on.

By the time of the canal's centenary in 1889, the prospects were distinctly unfavourable, and at the end of 1893 a notice was issued closing the canal east of Chalford until further notice. Regarded by many locally as an indication of imminent permanent closure, this episode stimulated the formation of a Trust consisting of six other canal companies and five local authorities. The sum of £18,000 was borrowed to finance major repair works and the entire canal length was re-opened in March 1899. Regrettably, this proved to be short-lived and the canal was closed at the summit three months later because of leakage.

These last few years of activity have left their mark on the canal for the towpath walker to detect today, particularly the next episode during the first decade of the twentieth century. Gloucestershire County Council, emerging from the demise of the Trust as the most involved party, took over the canals in 1900 and set about a further programme of repairs involving in places a concrete re-lining of the canal bed. The section from Cirencester to the Thames was re-opened in the following year, the Stroud to Daneway length the next year and the summit level in January 1904. However, lengthy periods of closure for repairs in each of the next three years proved too great a strain, and a further closure of twelve weeks for the complete rebuilding at Puck Mill Lower Lock and the pound above in 1907 probably proved decisive in the minds of long suffering councillors, who had taken a considerable risk with this project from the outset.

So, the end was in sight; the records show the last loaded boat (with stone) passing over the summit in May 1911, and thereafter only spasmodic repair work is recorded up to the outbreak of the First World War. By 1927 when closure notices were issued from Whitehall Bridge for the summit and eastern sections, and again in 1933 for the remainder of the canal, there can have been little real objection to the inevitable demise of the through link from Severn to Thames. And so it faded into obscurity and memory, and another forty years were to pass before serious restoration proposals were once again being canvassed in Gloucestershire for the 'greatest object of internal navigation in this kingdom'.

2 Building and Running the 'Great Undertaking'

Superlatives were the order of the day when the Thames & Severn canal was opened. With the press referring to the 'greatest object of internal navigation', the way was clear for correspondents to add their own praise, and with no less colourful writing. A contribution 'by an Englishman' to the *Gentleman's Magazine* (no. 60, 1790, 388-92) offers compliments on 'this great and stupendous undertaking', which had even attracted a visit from the King as the works were being completed. A correspondent to the *Bath Chronicle* (26 November 1789) waxed lyrical:

> *Friday November 20 1789*
> *Sir*
> *Yesterday a marriage took place between* Madam Sabrina, *a lady of Cambrian extraction and mistress of very extensive property in Montgomeryshire, (where she was born) and counties of Salop, Stafford and Worcester and Gloucester, and* Mr Thames, *commonly called Father Thames, a native of Gloucestershire, now a merchant trading from the city of London to all parts of the known world. The ceremony took place at Lechlade, by special licence, in the presence of hundreds of admiring spectators, with myself, who signed as witnesses – from whence the happy pair went to breakfast at Oxford; dine at London, and consummate at Gravesend; where the venerable Neptune, his whole train of inferior deities and nymphs, with his wife Venus, and her train, are to fling the stocking. An union which presages many happy consequences, and a numerous offspring. – I mention the lady's name, as the tendre came from her, after many struggles with her modesty and Cambrian aversion to a Saxon spouse.*
> *'A Traveller'*

This personification of the rivers into Madam Sabrina and Father Thames was oft repeated, and there remains a direct link between this association and the two niches in the Coates end of the Sapperton Tunnel, itself the major achievement of the whole enterprise, which it might fondly be believed were intended to house statues of these two symbols of union. In fact the assumption and the reference was enough; the image had been created and need not actually be executed in stone. As far as the records have been pursued, there is no evidence that either statue was made to complement or complete this portal; its classical balance was sufficient for the purpose.

Such contemporary accounts – both in the press and in more formal but no doubt more accurate terms in the official records – offer a rich source of information as to how the canal was built, by whom, under what instruction and using what materials, and when. This chapter attempts to show something of their value, especially when read alongside the detailed analyses and assessments which canal historians and scholars such as Humphrey Household and Charles Hadfield have provided, and of which good use has been made in the summary account below.

1633-1668

Suggestions to join the Severn and the Thames go back to the reign of Queen Elizabeth. Certainly by the early seventeenth century various ideas were being expounded; Henry Briggs made suggestions between 1619 and 1630. In May 1633, a Mr Hill, with his eye on the route through Stroud, petitioned King Charles I offering to find the best route between Severn and Thames and to estimate the cost of a navigation cut. Francis Mathew was another persistent advocate for improving and joining rivers. Three Bills were introduced in Parliament between 1662 and 1668 but none succeeded. Five possible routes were being explored.

1668-1775

Although no more bills were presented for over a century, the proposition never lacked an advocate and the project came to be appreciated as an economically valuable objective. The prosperity of the Stroud woollen industry between 1690 and 1760 acted as a powerful magnate for the Frome valley route, which attracted one of its greatest supporters in Allen, the first Earl Bathurst, whose pioneering achievements in the landscaping of Cirencester Park forms an integral part of the story of the canal's development. He was one of its principal advocates, suggesting 'that the junction of the two rivers under Sapperton Hill should be the crowning features of his splendid Cirencester Park' (source: Household 1969,19). It was Bathurst, as patron, working with Alexander Pope, as poet, who together put this into words, Pope writing to a friend in 1722 of Bathurst's dream that the Rivers Thames and Severn should be led to 'celebrate their Marriage in the midst of an immense Amphitheatre which would be the Admiration of Posterity'. So Bathurst supported the Stroudwater navigation bill in 1730 and suggested its extension to Cirencester if the bill were passed. The Earl died in September 1775, by which time construction of the Stroudwater had begun at Framilode; he was only a few years short of seeing his dream come to reality.

1779

Other observers made the point that any new navigation could only be successful economically if the condition of the two great rivers themselves were improved. Writing in his *New History of Gloucestershire* (1779) the historian Samuel Rudder was very perceptive of subsequent history when he observed of the Thames at Lechlade that:

> *The last mentioned river is navigable at this place for barges of forty or fifty tons burthen, but the want of water one part of the year, and long continued floods at other times, render the navigation extremely uncertain, and notwithstanding it leads to the metropolis, 'tis not so beneficial to the town as might be supposed, because it cannot be depended on for the general conveyance.*
>
> *The junction of this river with the Severn has been long talked of, but the execution of that project, on a good plan, is rather to be wished than expected. A late application to parliament on behalf of the Stroud-water canal, brought this scheme anew into contemplation, and the country was slightly surveyed in the year 1775, in order to extend the canal from Stroud to Cricklade, where the Thames is first navigable; but what purpose can such a junction answer, unless the navigation of that river were improved?*

The long struggle the Thames & Severn company experienced with the condition of the upper Thames and the eventual emergence of alternative canal routes to avoid it above Abingdon are all presaged in this wise comment.

1781

With the opening of the Stroudwater Navigation from the Severn at Framilode up to Stroud on 24 July 1779, the way was clear to press ahead with proposals for its extension eastwards, as Rudder indicated, and a meeting in support of the Thames & Severn Canal was held at the King's Head in Cirencester on 17 September 1781. A committee was formed, a subscription list opened and the momentum started to build. Some of the principal advocates were not themselves local to the county, but rather promoters and principals of the Staffordshire & Worcestershire Canal which had linked the Staffordshire and other West Midlands coalfields to the Severn at Stourport in 1772. Much of their driving initiative behind the Thames & Severn project was clear from the start, a desire to reach London with the coal and other products of the west midlands and to do so via the Severn, at a time when more direct routes from the midlands by canal did not yet exist. That such links were made soon after the Thames & Severn itself opened (via the Oxford Canal particularly) is an indication of the competitive edge which must have driven the whole project forward. Such initiatives aimed to break the hold Tyneside coal-owners had on supplies to London via the sea route.

1782

An anonymous publication *Considerations on the Idea of uniting the Rivers Thames and Severn through Cirencester with some observations on other Intended Canals* extolled the virtues of the route to Lechlade, and proved a timely contribution. In Cirencester on 22 December 1781 Robert Whitworth had been asked for his professional advice on the best route to choose; he visited the Cotswolds in October and completed his survey in December 1782. He was regarded as a surveyor and draughtsman of skill, with 'more experience in [levelling navigations] than any man of his profession'. However, the imprecise nature of his brief and the subsequent difficulties inherent in the assumptions he made have already been noted.

1783-1784

However, the issue was clear enough for a meeting of the promoters on 17 January 1783, once again at the King's Head in Cirencester, to adopt the Cirencester route and to introduce a Bill in the current session of Parliament. This was done by Sir William Guise MP on 20 February and obtained Royal Assent on 17 April. With the Act passed and the company set up, the first general assembly of the proprietors was held on 24 June.

Staff were appointed. One of the proprietors, Wolverhampton businessman James Perry, was appointed to personally supervise the building of the line, with an allowance of £400pa Josiah Clowes of Middlewich in Cheshire was appointed resident engineer at £300pa, or rather as 'Surveyor and Engineer and Head-Carpenter' to 'assist Mr Whitworth the Surveyor in setting out the Navigation'. In this relationship lay much of the success, but with no few problems, in the eventual construction of the line. Samuel Smith was clerk of works, at £120pa, with Richard Hall as his assistant. Hall was a local surveyor of repute, who had worked on the Stroudwater, checking levels before and after excavation and measuring the work of the canal cutters.

THAMES & SEVERN CANAL.

Notice is hereby given that on and after the 30th December, 1893, the portion of this Canal, extending from Chalford Chapel Pound at Bell Lock to the junction of the Navigation with the River Thames at Inglesham, and including the Branch Canal from Siddington to Cirencester, will be closed for through traffic, until further notice.

BY ORDER.

J. MAHON,

Clerk to the Company.

Paddington, London, 28th December, 1893.

Closure notice for the eastern end of the canal in 1893, the beginning of the end. (Courtesy Gloucestershire Record Office)

Starting in August 1783 Whitworth surveyed the nine-mile-long summit level including the line of Sapperton Tunnel, the most challenging part of the whole alignment. Clowes, Perry and others did much of the remainder. With the line marked, the company set out on the task of acquiring land, the acquisition of which was recorded in the 'Rough Plan' compiled by John Doyley, the London-based plan-surveyor to the company, which is in fact a leather bound volume of sixty-six pages of beautifully delineated maps. Such was the effect of the long-term desire to achieve this canal, that there was very little opposition from landowners along the route when the process of acquisition actually began.

A system of organising the labour force, described by Household as a gang-piecework system, was favoured, whereby gang leaders made individual agreements for each task to be undertaken. It might be argued that the impact of this can be seen along the line of the canal even today, where a detailed analysis of the surviving built heritage would show the essential variations in method and indeed of materials which delineates one contract (and one team) from another. This would make a fascinating study. Having divided the project up in this way, the company nevertheless wanted to put the entire task of driving the Sapperton Tunnel into the hands of one man, at a fixed piecework rate. In selecting Charles Jones, for whom Clowes provided one of the recommendations, it made a costly error of judgement. The story of the tunnel, the construction of which ran in parallel with the building of much of the remainder of the canal line, is summarised in Chapter 8.

1785-1788

Work had begun at Stroud, driving eastwards. On 31 January 1785 the first vessel entered the Wallbridge lock in Stroud, with the canal open as far as Chalford. By the summer of 1786 it had been completed up to Daneway Bridge. Supplies to the works in the tunnel could then be delivered to this point by canal and trade with the countryside around developed. Much of the activity of the following two years is dominated by the construction of the tunnel, most of which had been completed by midsummer 1788 when King George III visited in company with Earl Bathurst. He is likely to have visited both portals. Meanwhile cutting the remainder of the line had continued steadily eastwards. The summit level from the entrance of the tunnel to Siddington, together with the Cirencester arm, had been completed by 1787 and work continued on the long eastern section towards the Thames.

1789

Apart from the cutting of the canal, buildings were being erected, the principal group being at the new Brimscombe Port, where the main Port House, a combined office, headquarters and warehouse and the work of Thomas Cook, had a keystone dated 1789. It can be assumed that the other three principal wharfhouses, all built to the same style, also date from 1789 or shortly afterwards.

The completion of the works and opening of the canal caused much celebration in print as well as along the canal line. Some of it almost incidentally provides very useful information on the process as well as the outcome.

> *On the 20th April 1789, Mr Joseph [sic] Clowes, the operative engineer, passed this tunnel, for the first time, in a vessel of 30 tons. Inclosed I send you an elegant engraving of each entrance; they have been made at the expence of the Company, and are affixed as ornaments to their mortgage instruments.*
> [*Gentleman's Magazine*, 60 (1790), 388-392]

Are these illustrations perhaps the same ones used on the company's share certificates (colour picture no.3)?

With the tunnel open, the trading operations could move ever eastwards and reports of the impact of such activity continued to be of interest in the press in the early years of the canal's operation. In this extract, the public advantages too obvious to need enumeration included a reduction in the price of coal which a correspondent in the following year to the *Gentleman's Magazine* (60, 1790, 109-10) noted had dropped from 24*s* to 18*s* per ton in Cirencester and 32 or 33*s* to 22*s* per ton in Lechlade.

The Port of Cirencester

On Wednesday 22nd April, four barges laden with coals, brought from the Severn, after having passed through the grand subterraneous trunk under Sapperton Hill and Hagley [Hailey] Wood, arrived in Cirencester in Gloucestershire. How welcome such a sight must be in a country where fuel has been hitherto not only dear but scarce, may easily be imagined, and the inhabitants of Cirencester testified by public rejoicings their gladness on the occasion. Thousands of spectators lined the banks of the canal to witness the novel scene, expressing their joy and surprise on seeing

a river brought to, and a port formed on, the high wolds of Gloucestershire. Other loaded barges went forward for Kempsford, to which place the canal is completed, and we hear that in a short time it will be in or over the Thames, in its direction to Oxford etc. The public advantages that must result from this noble undertaking are too obvious to need enumeration.
[*Gloucestershire Notes & Queries* vol. IV (1890), no. 1805, page 445 reporting 'the following scrap of intelligence from Cirencester.....published in the newspapers a hundred years ago']

Before the end of that month, the canal was opened to within three miles of Inglesham. The deliberations about where to make the link with the Thames caused some last-minute differences of viewpoint, before the approved parliamentary line to Inglesham was adopted in May and the remaining section cut through, although not before the evidence of such deliberation (or perhaps miscalculation?) had been left for all to see at Dudgrove double lock. Meanwhile, other reports had noted coal being carried to Kempsford on 28 April. Finally, the junction with the Thames was made on 14 November (the date inscribed upon the bridge at Inglesham) and the first vessel passed laden into the river on 19 November 1789. Within a month the first landings of Staffordshire coal were being made at Lechlade wharf, with due celebrations. The canal including the tunnel had been constructed in 6½ years, a remarkable achievement by any standards, and it was at this point that *The Times* and other journals produced the 'greatest object of internal navigation' story.

1790

However, the joy was short-lived and the Thames & Severn quickly experienced one of its greatest problems, which was to remain throughout its life as a working waterway – the disruption to through trade caused by the necessary closure of any one section or structure. The tunnel was closed for three months in 1790 and again for several weeks in 1791 for repairs to leaks. There were also the continuing problems about the state of the River Thames especially in its upper reaches, where navigation was difficult, and this was to prove a long-standing and significant issue.

In its early days, when the company saw itself as both owner of and a principal operator along the system, it had over 200 staff all along its line. Other than the seventeen or so at Brimscombe, there was a clerk of works at Cirencester or Siddington, a staff of four at Thames Head, agents at the principal wharves of Wallbridge, Siddington, Cricklade, Kempsford and Lechlade, and twelve watchmen. These latter were the eyes and ears of the operation, with specific maintenance and security responsibilities for defined sections of the line, hence their other name of lengthmen.

Watchmen were located at Stroud, Brimscombe, Chalford, Puck Mill, Sapperton, Coates Field, Furzenleaze, Cirencester, South Cerney, Cerney Wick, Marston Meysey and Inglesham. At five of these the distinctive roundhouses were built (Chalford, Coates, Cerney Wick, Marston Meysey and Inglesham) and less obvious but equally functional rectangular cottages at Sapperton (by the tunnel entrance) and Furzenleaze (and later at Wilmoreway and Eisey). The role of lock-keeper was assumed to form part of the watchman's duties, as at South Cerney.

The navigation was open from 5.00 a.m. to 9.00 p.m. in summer and 6.00 a.m. to 6.00 p.m. in winter months.

1792

The Thames Head Pump was opened to increase water supplies and Boxwell Spring lock was constructed as a means of improving water retention in this eastern section.

1810

The Kennet & Avon and the Wilts & Berks Canals were opened.

1813

The company purchased Parkend Wharf at Lechlade to improve its operations at the eastern end of the canal.

1816

A committee, with responsibilities to the City of London for the Thames Navigation, gathered information on the state of the river which they showed to be in poor condition. They also indicated that the Thames & Severn was 'defective on account of the weeds' and 'the decayed state of some of the lock gates'. Loss of water was a major problem right from the outset and such poor maintenance made matters worse.

1819

The opening in April of the 8½-mile North Wilts Canal formed a link between the Thames & Severn and the Wilts & Berks, with a junction at Latton Basin, and so provided an alternative route cutting off the upper reaches of the River Thames above Abingdon.

Contractors hard at work at the Daneway entrance to Sapperton Tunnel c.1903 in the early years of Gloucestershire County Council ownership of the canal. Here clay is being crushed for use in the canal bed whilst the tunnel is blocked off by wooden stop-planks.

1820-1831

Water shortages and other defects had become such a problem that specialist contractors Hugh and David McIntosh were brought in to advise. The result was an extensive programme of overhaul and improvement over the following quarter-century which raised the whole operation into what Household described as 'a high state of efficiency'. Interestingly the ground survey which David McIntosh made only covered the line from Stroud to Latton, suggesting that the route newly opened via the North Wilts and Wilts & Berks was the preferred (or most practical) option from that date. Narrow boats could easily use this route, and had begun to oust the traditional river craft for which the Thames & Severn had been designed. The opening of the Gloucester & Berkeley Canal in 1827 increased the pressure of competition.

Re-puddling was done in various places, locks were thoroughly overhauled (eight new pairs of gates in 1822 alone) and the system of side ponds introduced, wide shallow basins capable of storing and recycling up to a third or more of the water from each lock usage. The notoriously difficult five upper locks at Daneway were improved in this way, probably in 1823, but the equally problematic lower lock at Wilmoreway was not improved until 1831 when a new cottage was also built for the watchman, moved here from Cerney Wick. Meanwhile in 1824 an attempt was made to synchronise all the neighbouring canals' maintenance work into an annual Whitsun stoppage; this was only partially successful. The other significant conservation measure, of shortening the locks, was not introduced until 1841. The story of the Thames Head pump and its improvements over the years should also be seen as part of the improvements at this time. In January 1831 'a tremendous leakage broke out' at Bluehouse which 'lowered the summit 5 inches'.

1841-1842

Seventeen locks through the Golden Valley, and then seven at Siddington and South Cerney were shortened about 20ft as a means of saving water. By building a new arch across the upper chamber and re-hanging the gates, the length of the lock was reduced to 70ft from 90ft and some 20% of the water saved. This greatly improved the efficiency of the system.

However, railway competition began to make its mark with the completion of the line from Swindon to Cirencester, opened on 31 May 1841. Paradoxically, its construction helped to give the canal business, in the short term, the maximum tonnage on the Thames & Severn of 89,271 tons being carried in 1841. By comparison, forty years later this was reduced to 43,811 tons. The railway was extended through to Gloucester in 1845.

1845

Introduction of the boat-weighing gauge at Brimscombe Port.

1853-1854

Installation of the Cornish engine at Thames Head pumping station, replacing the older Boulton & Watt engine installed in 1792; by working round the clock it could deliver some three million gallons of water each day into the canal. Its installation marked the end of the period of structural improvements to the canal which date back to the survey of 1820.

1866

An attempt was made to convert the canal into a railway (see below for 1882).

1870s

Examples of the problems of low water on the canal affecting traffic; an inspection in October 1875 showed that no boat with a draught of more than 2ft 6in could pass the summit level. Other parts of the through route such as the Wilts & Berks Canal were in no better state.

1877

Ice from Norway

> *Messrs Cole & Lewis, of the Cotswold Bacon Factory [Cirencester], have just imported from Norway 300 tons of ice, for bacon curing. The ice is now lying in Sharpness Docks and will be conveyed to Cirencester via the Thames & Severn Canal.*
> [*Wilts & Gloucestershire Standard* 28 April 1877, p5]

1882

Another attempt to convert the line of the canal into a railway, all part of the competition between railway companies to secure through routes. A previous attempt had been made in 1866. One outcome of such railway politics was the acquisition of the canal (through nominees) by the Great Western Railway on 11 May 1882. Another was the group of Allied Navigations, formed in 1895 to resist the railway conversion proposals for the Thames & Severn.

1885-1886

With continuing problems of leakage on the summit, it was estimated that some 60% of the water pumped at Thames Head was lost. Economy measures included the dismissal of several lock-keepers during the winter of 1885-1886, and of one of the two engine keepers at Thames Head.

1888-1892

Concerns about declining trade were reported in the press. In Cirencester, the annual reports of Mr Williams, the Sanitary Inspector to the Local Board, provide valuable insights e.g:

The Canal Boats

> *The number of separate vessels during the year has been 17, making 94 trips, as their cargoes consist chiefly of Bristol road stone, sawdust, bricks, and gravel, some of the boats load back with timber. They are most of them old boats. Several old vessels without cabins have been used lashed to the canal boats, thus a load of 20 tons may be divided into two or three parts, what is called the "Summit" not having sufficient water to float a fair cargo, and many times a part of a load of stones has to be left at Sapperton, the boatman having to go back and fetch what he has left behind. There was no boat in January or May, five in June, one in July, three in August, and four in September. The canal is not at all improved, nor its business. I have only seen three women and one child in the boats during the year, these women being the wives of the boatmen, with whom they travel, and work as men.*
> [*Wilts & Glos Standard* 28 January 1888 p5]

Looking up the Siddington flight of locks in 1896, from just above the bottom lock. All is in decay, with little sign of activity. The Midland & South Western Junction Railway line crosses the picture. (Photo courtesy Hugh McKnight Collection)

> *The traffic on the canal has been still less this year than last, indeed it seems almost wholly diverted to the railways. I have only seen seven boats, making 24 trips. The difficulty is the want of water to bring up sufficient load to pay. I have seen no child and only one woman during the year. If the boats have anything like a load they are obliged to lighten at Siddington and go back and fetch what they left behind. The men say they can scarcely earn one shilling per day each, water being so short. There has been plenty of water the last weeks, but no traffic, it having been diverted to the railways.*
> [*Wilts & Glos Standard* 30 January 1892, p4]

1893

The Thames and Severn Canal
We hear that the whole of the officials and others employed on the canal have received a fortnight's notice to leave. [*Wilts & Glos Standard* 23 December 1893, p4]

The closure notice was issued from Paddington on 28 December, giving two days' notice of closure of the entire line east of Chalford Chapel Lock to Inglesham as from 30 December 'to through traffic, until further notice'. Even in the busiest years of the Thames & Severn some 43% of all traffic was confined to the western end; this had grown to perhaps two-thirds of all traffic by this stage, producing incidentally over half of the earnings derived for the company. Hence the cut-off point at Chalford.

1894

A detailed assessment of the state of the canal undertaken for the Allied Navigations estimated an expenditure of £10,309 for its restoration.

1895

A Thames & Seven Canal Trust was set up to put the canal into order. Five navigations (Severn Commissioners, the Sharpness, the Stroudwater, the Staffs & Worcs and the Wilts & Berks companies) joined with six public bodies to form the trust. Works of improvement were also underway on the upper Thames, to aid the development of through traffic. A programme of work began on refurbishing and upgrading the canal, sections of which were re-opened as the work progressed, for example the section up to Daneway by the beginning of 1898.

1896

A useful photographic record of some fifteen photographs was taken on a tour of the canal by Henry Rodolph de Salis, member of a family long connected with canals and himself a director of a major carrying company, Fellows Morton & Clayton Ltd. He sought greater efficiency on the canals and in the course of eleven years travelled some 14,000 miles carrying out investigations. One result was his systematic survey which was first published as *Bradshaw's Canals And Navigable Rivers of England and Wales* in 1904, a useful handbook of information and statistics. He visited the Thames & Severn in 1896 in his boat *Dragonfly*, and a photograph survives of it moored up in Latton basin. His evidence showed the canal in poor condition; at least two boats were shown as trapped along its length for want of water, one in the locks below Daneway and the other in the pound above the locks at South Cerney.

A memorable event, recorded here between Upper and Lower Wallbridge locks in Stroud on 11 April 1899, celebrating a re-opening of the through canal line. The longboat Trial *is returning to Stonehouse from London with a cargo of wool for Charles Hooper & Sons, mill-owners of Eastington. Her round trip took three weeks and was recorded in a pamphlet published for the occasion. Stroud Brewery buildings are in the background; the Stroudwater company's headquarters building is to the right.*(Photo courtesy Humphrey Household)

Cutting clay for use in re-puddling the canal at Bluehouse on the notoriously leaky summit level, c.1903/1904. (Photo Henry Taunt of Oxford, courtesy Centre for Oxfordshire Studies, copyright Oxfordshire County Council)

1899

The canal was re-opened throughout on 15 March. In celebration, the narrow boat *The Trial* brought goods from London, its journey recorded in a printed leaflet 'April 1899. From London to Eastington by Water'. However the canal was open for only about three months before leaks on the summit forced closure again in June. These extended over about three miles eastwards from the tunnel entrance at Coates. An article in *The Engineer* in December 1898 had remarked of the summit that 'it is doubtful whether there is any portion of canal in England more troublesome to keep water-tight than this has been.'

1900-1911

Gloucestershire County Council, a key member of the Trust, assumed management of the canal from 8 January 1900 under a Warrant of Abandonment from the former proprietors, which was confirmed by Act of Parliament on 2 July 1901. Such acquisition of a canal by a recently-formed local authority was an interesting and risky exercise in public expenditure at this date, as it was to prove. A programme of remedial works was undertaken, including concrete lining the King's Reach and re-puddling a three-mile stretch along this part of the summit. The programme of works progressed so that the length from Cirencester to the Thames was re-opened by July 1902, from the western end up to Daneway by April 1903 and the remainder of the summit by January 1904. The narrow boat *Staunch* was the first vessel to pass over the summit, on 3 March 1904, delivering coal to Cirencester.

Optimism was still in the air. The author of *Bradshaw's Canals and Navigable Rivers* of 1904 (a bible of canal information) 'confidently expected that the additional works which have been executed by the County Council will in future enable the traffic on the canal to be maintained without interruption'. However, despite the celebrations for the journey of *Staunch*, it proved an isolated occasion. Very little traffic had passed over the summit in the ten years before the *Staunch*, and very little afterwards despite the programme of repairs. Puck Mill pound was re-puddled in 1907, the last of this particular series of works, and closures continued to be necessary to deal with leakages on the summit and elsewhere.

The Sanitary Inspector for Cirencester Urban District Council's Annual Report stated:

> *The portion of the canal in the district has been available for use at intervals during the year. A few visits have been made by Stroud boats for cargoes of timber and formal inspections of two boats employed in this work were made near the close of the year and found satisfactory.*
> [*Wilts & Glos Standard* 1 February 1908, p5]

Worse was to follow as the consulting engineer G.W. Keeling reported to the County Council in February 1909:

> *I am of the opinion that it will cost quite £100 per mile per annum (£3,000pa) for management and maintenance to keep the Canal open in a sufficiently efficient condition for traffic. …. the difficulty of the navigation is the want of an adequate water supply by gravitation to the summit, involving pumping, which in itself is a serious expense to a navigation with little traffic.*

On the summit level at Furzenleaze, contractors are re-puddling sections of canal; Bluehouse, the watchman's cottage, is on the right. The date is 1903/1904 during a concerted restoration campaign. (Photo Henry Taunt of Oxford, courtesy Gloucestershire Record Office, copyright Oxfordshire County Council)

Dereliction at Upper Siddington in 1923. One of the bottom gates has collapsed, as seen through the bridge arch. This is the very eastern end of the nine-mile-long summit level. (Photo Frank Lloyd, courtesy and copyright British Waterways Archives, Gloucester, ref 5258)

Later that same year the Thames Conservancy's engineer inspected the whole canal line (except the tunnel) and came up with some even more startling figures. Apart from over £8,000 worth of immediate expenditure required (and three times more than Keeling had estimated above), concrete lining of other sections badly in need of such protection would cost £24,500 and a further option to build concrete walls throughout the canal as a way to retain water would require an additional expenditure a few pounds short of £73,000. None of this was done or even seriously contemplated.

What turned out to be a final effort for the summit and eastern sections occurred with the passage of a boat with twenty-four tons of grain (one of the few commodities which did pass over the whole canal line from time to time) to Kempsford and Lechlade in April 1911. The last recorded carriage of goods was twenty tons of stone the following month, on 11 May 1911.

1912-1933

Most of the staff were discharged east of Chalford in 1912, and the long decline set in with little or no trade through that area. The adventures of leisure seekers did however add some colour at this time (see Chapter 3) until closure east of Whitehall Bridge in the Golden Valley was announced for 31 January 1927. A detailed report to the County Council in 1924 had paved the way for this. Despite other issues, such as the rest of the canal remaining open as a flood water channel, it too was closed by an Order dated 9 June 1933, concluding the remaining trading activities in the valley, the final years of which have happily been recorded in photographs and reminiscences. Canal land and buildings were sold off, maintenance was withdrawn and a period of some forty years followed during which the Thames & Severn Canal became increasingly little more than memory and the source of anecdote and recollection.

The coal barge Staunch *arrives at Cirencester*

- The Re-Opened Thames and Severn Canal
- Staffordshire to Cirencester by Water
- Cruise of the Coal Barge *Staunch*

There is a popular lyric, of which a localised version is extant, whose numerous stanzas, set to a not exceedingly exhilarating melody, describe in picturesque detail the various and startling incidents in "The Cruise of the Calabar". Now, the 'Calabar' was a clipper boat, copper fastened fore and aft, she is said to have sailed the placid waters of the Thames and Severn Canal, and to have been capable of at least "two knots an hour", and, in fact, she was averred to be "the fastest boat on the whole canal, though only one 'oss power." We have not the poem at hand, but we have a vivid memory of the manifold dangers that beset the devoted craft, as thus:

> And when she came to Tunnel House,
> A very dangerous part,
> She ran bow on to a lump of coal
> Which wasn't marked down in the chart.

The song also describes how neatly the ship weathered "the straits of Smerrel Bridge, where you can't pass two at a time", while still more thrilling was her escape from the rascally pirates who essayed her capture, but to whom she showed a clean pair of heels, thanks to the energy of all hands thus stimulated by her heroic commander:

> "Put on full steam," the Captain cried,
> "For we are sorely pressed."
> And the Engineer from the bank replied
> That "th' 'oss was a doin' 'is best."

Well, the good barge *Staunch* (owner and captain, Joseph Fletcher, from the port of New Swindon, and a native of the famous inland shipping resort of Chalford) has not the stirring adventures of the Calabar to recount, but she has been traversing the same classic waterway, and on Tuesday last she made the port of Cirencester with a cargo of some 37 tons of Staffordshire coal – the first consignment of water-borne coal that has reached the town for we are afraid to say how many years. The cargo was brought to the order of Messrs. F. Gegg and Co., coal merchants, of Cirencester, whose business is conducted at the Canal Wharf, and who therefore determined to charter a trial trip on the re-opened canal.

Captain Joseph Hewer, to whom belongs the honour of re-inaugurating what it may be hoped will be a considerable coal traffic on the old and historic waterway, has been in the boat business all his life. His father, Mr Francis Hewer, of Chalford, broke him in when he was about seven years old, and when business on the Thames and Severn canal fell off, owing to its increasingly dilapidated condition and the consequent difficulty of navigation, he betook himself to New Swindon, and for 12 or 15 years he had four boats regularly plying between that place and Bristol. But three years ago the Wilts and Berks Canal also became unnavigable, and although Captain Hewer had plenty of work – Messrs Butt and Skurray, the millers, were willing to keep him regularly employed – he had to seek other occupation, and though he did not actually burn his boats, he broke up two, sold a third, and retained the fourth, appropriately named the *Staunch*. Naturally he looks back with regret to the interruption of his old calling – "I should have been a hundred pound better off to-day if the Wilts and Berks Canal had kept going" – but, being an experienced "old salt", if of the freshwater variety, he kept his weather eye open, and seeing that his boat was becoming more and more hopelessly stranded, he fifteen months ago headed her for the Thames and Severn Canal via Latton, attracted thither by the restoration works in progress. For ten months the *Staunch* lay up at Latton Wharf, but two months ago she once more kissed her native waters. By way of testing her capabilities in a "sea way", she carried some gravel from Cerney to Cirencester for Messrs. Gegg and Co., and some hundred tons of road stone from Siddington to Cerney Wick, and a month ago she entered on her Staffordshire voyage. Sailing "light" to Gloucester, she there took up a load of timber baulks, which she carried to Old Hill, near Dudley, and then went some 25 miles further on to the Hednesford Colliery, Staffordshire, to embark Messrs. Gegg and Co.'s load of coal.

The homeward voyage was begun on Wednesday morning in last week, the following several systems of navigation having to be traversed:

Birmingham Canal	30	miles
Worcester Canal	30	miles
Severn (Worcester to Gloucester)	29.5	miles
Berkeley Canal	8	miles
Stroudwater Canal	6	miles
Thames and Severn Canal	17	miles
	= 120.5	miles

Like the Calabar, the *Staunch* is a boat of one horse power and Captain Hewer's single horse hauled the *Staunch* to Staffordshire and back unaided, including the Severn stretch, which is sometimes accomplished by means of a tug. The 120 miles were covered in five and half working days, divided by the following stopping places: 1st day, Birmingham; 2nd day, Hambury Wharf, near Droitwich; 3rd day, Tewkesbury; 4th day, Dudbridge, Stroud, where the "Staunch" lay up for the Sunday; 5th day, Tunnel House, Coates; 6th day (10 o'clock), Cirencester Wharf. The fifth day was no child's play, for 29 locks had to be negotiated between Dudbridge and Coates, two of them on the Stroudwater Canal, and 27 on the Thames and Severn in the ascent from the valley to the summit level, and the dark recesses of the Sapperton tunnel had to be penetrated. The tunnel, nearly 2.5 miles in length, was got through in three and a quarter hours, the boat being propelled by means of tunnel sticks manipulated by Captain Hewer and his "mate", Richard Bentley. The canal was found to be in capital order throughout, including the tunnel, and at no point was there the slightest difficulty with the heavily loaded boat drawing 3 feet 7 inches of water. The tunnel Hewer found to be greatly improved as compared with his former experience of it, and the influx of water through the roof at Caseywell is much reduced.

As regards the commercial aspects of the undertaking, Captain Hewer accepted the charter at the same rate as that charged by the railway companies, viz., 7s 6d per ton, so that assuming his load to be 37 tons his freight would come to £13 17s 6d. The tolls he had to pay to the several navigations traversed amounted to between £5 and £6, and the balance is what is available for labour, horse and other expenses, use of boat, etc. What is needed, of course, to make the venture successful is the development of a traffic in round timber to pay for the outwards voyage.

We believe Mr E.N. Edmonds has had a cargo of corn carried to Kempsford; Mr G. Durnell of Watermoor, has had several cargoes of timber; and last Sunday a boat with 24 tons of road stone, carrier Mr Barnes, reached Kempsford from the Gloucester end. Mr P.J. Trouncer, of Chester Lodge, has this week placed an electric launch upon the canal.

[Source: Wilts & Gloucestershire Standard 26 March 1904, p5]

Staunch unloading coal at Cirencester wharf on 19 March 1904. The local coal merchant Frank Gegg has utilised every available vehicle, including three delivery carts plus a fine four-wheeled farm wagon. The cargo was thirty-seven tons of Staffordshire coal, well above the normal loading, even for waterways in good condition. (Photo courtesy Humphrey Household)

3 Leisure and Pleasure

Although canals were not originally intended or indeed built for leisure purposes, there is a long history of such use well before the development of the vast and growing canal leisure industry which sustains the network today, and which lies behind the enormous and exciting programme of restoration initiatives across the country being launched (with some already completed) at the beginning of the twenty-first century. At first such investigations on the ground were driven more by curiosity than relaxation, and the obvious geographical and landscape attractions of routes such as the Thames & Severn, crossing the great divide between one great river system and another, could not avoid being the subject of curiosity, enquiry, exploration and enjoyment. This process is in fact as old as the suggestions for creating the navigation itself, beginning in the seventeenth century and still alive and well today. This is not to say that canal journeying was necessarily pleasant; obstructions, added to the hard work of passing through locks, created both challenge and no doubt frustration. This selection of examples shows not only something of the activity itself but also the flavour in which it was reported or set down for the record.

1641

Only eight years after Mr Hill's petition of May 1633 John Taylor, born at Gloucester in 1578 and known as the 'water-poet', took a boat up the Thames and Churn almost to Cirencester, carted it across the watershed and, armed 'with a hatchett', forced his way down the Frome to the Severn. He wrote exuberant descriptions for a ready market, but also had a serious interest in transport and was a confirmed believer in the value of inland navigation. So although not thinking primarily in terms of leisure, his exploits might read today almost as if they were. The content of his account is worth the struggle to read it!

> John Taylor's Last Voyage, and Adventure, *Performed from the twentieth of July last 1641, to the tenth of September following. In which time he past, with a Scullers Boate from the cittie of London, to the cities and Townes of Oxford, Gloucester, Shrewesbury, Bristoll, Bathe, Monmouth and Hereford.*
>
> *Thurseday the twenty seaven, I passed with my Boate from Abington to Oxford, where I was well entertained with good cheere and worshipfull company at University Colledge; The next day I passed to a place called Bablack Hive (or Hithe). And on Thursday the twenty nine, I passed by Lechlad, and came to Creeklad; This towne of Creeklad is five miles distant by land from Ciciter, but it is easier to row sixtie miles by water on the River of Thames, then it is to passe betweene those two townes, for there are so many milles, fords and shallowes with stops, and other impediments that a whole daies hard labour with my selfe, and foure more could neyther by toyle or Art get but to a Mill of one Master Hortones at a place called Suddington, a mile short of Ciciter, so that according to land measure we went but foure miles in a long dayes travel. The last of July I left Suddington Mill, with the honest welcome of the Miller and his wife, and with much a doe for want of water I gatt to Ciciter, where the River*

was so dry that it would beare my boate no further; at the hither end of that Towne there stands a great Barne belonging to one Cooke, of whom I hired a Waine, wherein I put my Boate my selfe and my Men, Boyes, and luggage; this Waine did in lesse then five houres draw me from the River Isis neere Ciciter, to a brooke called Stroud, which brooke hath it's head or Spring in Bessley Hundred neere Misserden in Cotswould in Glostershire, (Stowd and Churne might be cut into one, and so Severne & Thames might by made almost joined friends) are within 4. miles of Churne, which hath its first spring nere Coberley, 7 miles from Glocester & falles into Isis about Lechlad, so that 4 miles cutting in the Land betwixt Churne and Stroud, would be a meanes to make passages from Thames to Severne, to Wye, to both the Rivers of Avon in England, and to one River of Avon in Monmouthshire, which falles into the River of Uske neere Carlion in Wales. By which meanes goods might be conveyed by water too & from London, in Rivers at cheape rates without danger, almost to half the countyes in England and Wales. But there is a devil or two called sloth and couvetuousnesse, that are the bane of all good endeavours and laudable Actions, but more of this shall be said hereafter.

I being uncarted (with my boate) at a place called Stonehouse, in the Afforesaid brooke called Stroud, with passing and wading, with haling over high bankes at fulling Milles (where there are many) with plucking over suncke trees, over and under strange Bridges, of wood and stone, and in some places the brooke was scarce as broad as my Boate, I being oftentimes impeached with the bowghes and branches of willowes and Alder Trees, which grew so thicke, hanging over and into the brooke, so that the day light or Sunne could scarce peepe through the branches, that in many places all passages were stop'd; so that I was sometimes forced to cut and hew out my way with a hatchet; with this miserable toyle all the day I gat at night to a Mill called Froombridge Mill, whereas (for our comfort) was neither Victualing house, meate, drinke or lodging, but that a good gentlewoman, one Mistress Bowser, there did comisetare our wants, and though she were not accustomed to victual or lodge Travellers, yet the rarety of our boate, and strangeness of my adventure moved her so farre that shee at an easie rate did furnish us with good dyet, my selfe with a bed in an out-house, and my men and boyes with a sweet new mowed and new made hayloft.

[In the Gloucestershire Collection: *Works of John Taylor*, 1870-1878, 5 vols (in 4); see volume 2 (5), Last Voyage]

1792-1828

With the canal open, a number of artists had an additional reason to study the upper reaches of the Thames, a river which always held considerable attraction. In this period at least four books published on the Thames include illustrations of the canal. Samuel Ireland's *Picturesque Views on the River Thames* (1792) is the most informative and is based on sketches made in the summer of 1790, in the very first year of the canal's operation (see colour picture no.2). Perhaps the most artistic is Joseph Farington, RA with views of Thames Head and Inglesham roundhouse (see colour picture no.5) in W. Coombe's *An History of the River Thames* of 1794. Fuller descriptions are available in William Bernard Cooke's *The Thames* (1811), who showed that curious travellers could go through the tunnel in a boat specially kept for the purpose at Coates. W. Westall and S. Owen's *Picturesque Tour of the River Thames* (1828) is also informative (see for example **117**), whilst *Delineations of Gloucestershire* published in 1816 with plates engraved by J. & H.S. Storer and text by J.N. Brewer includes the fine illustration of Brimscombe Port (see **72**).

A canoeing trip along the Thames & Severn, coming down the South Cerney flight of locks and entering the bottom lock, c.1885. No further details are known. (Photo Henry Taunt of Oxford, courtesy Centre for Oxfordshire Studies, copyright Oxfordshire County Council)

In the summer of 1815 the poet Shelley together with Mary Godwin and two friends arrived at Inglesham; their plan was to travel to the Severn and then travel north on that river. However they discovered that transit of the canal would cost them £20, just as if they were a fully-laden barge. There was no capacity or flexibility in the system for tourists, harking back to the company's decision in 1794 that pleasure boats could only pass when one of their committee members was on board or written permission had been obtained.

1861

The *Wilts & Glos Standard* covered the whole of east Gloucestershire and adjoining north Wiltshire from its base in Cirencester (and still does) and so was able to report activity on the canal from the summit level to Lechlade and indeed beyond.

Skating feats
On Saturday last a gentleman of this town skated along the canal from Siddington to Cricklade, and from thence to Swindon, returning in same manner. On Monday three gentlemen skated from Swindon to Siddington on their way to Cirencester market, but they returned by railway. Some beautiful skating has been witnessed on the pond in the park, several ladies have taken part in this healthy and graceful exercise.
[12 January 1861, p8]

Diving skills on show at one of the flight of locks below Daneway; this is believed to be a group of Scouts from Woodchester. Swimming in locks along the canal was a popular pastime, and several were used for this purpose in and around Stroud. (Photo courtesy Howard Beard Collection; copy also in Corinium Museum Cirencester collection ref. 1988/136)

1868

In the summer months three men on a journey from Manchester to London were the first to record their experiences of travelling the canal, in a canoe and a skiff. Their account *The Waterway to London, as explored in the* Wanderer *and* Ranger *with sail, paddle and oar* etc (1869) records that their journey as far as Saul had been free of charges, as they had used no locks. However, charges were sought on the Stroudwater and more firmly at Wallbridge, where they negotiated terms to obtain a ticket to pass. Tourism did not seem to figure in the scheme of things even though they found the canal 'one of the most beautiful' they had experienced, and the journey through the tunnel memorable.

1876

Some journeys along the canal proved to be memorable for all the wrong reasons, including injury:

Narrow Escape from Drowning
On Thursday afternoon, as Master Walter MacGregor and Master C. Bingham were boating on the Thames and Severn Canal, near the Blue House, the former met with an accident which well nigh ended fatally. Each of the lads had a canoe, and on rounding a curve near the above point they met a barge coming in the opposite direction. Unfortunately they essayed to pass the

barge (which was nearly across the canal) upon different sides, and consequently Master MacGregor's canoe collided with the larger vessel, and he was turned over into the water. He sank, and on rising, his head came in contact with the bottom of the barge, and for some time he was unable to escape this terrible obstruction. Ultimately, he did so, and came to the surface in time to witness the preparation of formidable boat hooks, etc., which were about to be employed to effect his rescue. The canoe being righted, Master MacGregor safely accomplished the return journey, and beyond the wetting was uninjured.
[*Wilts & Glos. Standard* 23 September 1876 p5]

1888

In its edition of 29 September 1888, the *Wilts & Glos. Standard* carried an account of a through journey of the canal from west to east, including an interesting experience in the tunnel:

Canalising through Gloucestershire
On the following morning we started [from Brimscombe] about eleven and reached Sapperton about half past two. We stayed some time here for lunch and rest after a long chain of locks which brought us through the far famed Golden Valley. The scenery from Bradford to Bath and from Stonehouse to the tunnel is some of the finest in England and more resembling the banks of the Wye than any other part I can call to mind. At four o'clock we entered Sapperton Tunnel

Trips into the tunnel were popular and this group, believed to be from Brimscombe Polytechnic, must have been one of the last, sometime between 1910-1912. They are seen here emerging at the Daneway end. The 'tunnel sticks' used for propulsion can be seen, a practice firmly discouraged earlier in the life of the canal because of the damage caused to the stone and brickwork lining the tunnel. (Photo courtesy Gloucestershire Record Office)

wisely provided with two sticks and a horn lantern. The tunnel is 2 miles long and nowhere is it wide enough to permit of rowing. Two of us seated on the thwarts as in rowing pushed the boat along from the side with the sticks we had obtained at the inn whilst the third steered. This mode of progression is easy enough at first but during the last half mile the sticks seemed to grow remarkably heavy. About a mile from the entrance we became aware that we were not the only occupants of the tunnel. Shouts were heard echoing through the vault and the red light of a barge loomed ahead. On hearing it we shouted asking if there was room to pass.

'What beam?' was the reply.
'Four feet eight inches' was our trembling response.
'Oh you can pass anything anywhere.'

We were reassured. They were two barges being worked through and as their beam was only 7ft 1in we passed them easily and in the narrowest part. We were told that the tunnel was only eleven foot broad so we were afraid we should have to return. However, it must have been slightly more. In some places where it is cut out of solid rock it is much wider. Only beware of digging the sticks too high into the rock or shouting lest a piece fall upon your head. About halfway through a small spring escapes from the north side of the tunnel. You can hear it from a great distance but it is not formidable. Time occupied in going through the tunnel one hour four minutes including stoppage by barges. The country on leaving the mouth is unlovely. The first object of interest is the head water of the Thames which rises near a bridge trickling out of an old dyke, then another bridge and then the Cornish beam pumping engine which pumps the water of five springs into the summit level. Our stay that night was at Cirencester on a branch a good mile long leaving the Canal just above Siddington locks. The hotel at Cirencester is the King's Head, by far the best hotel we had stayed at and one of the most moderate. In the morning we left Cirencester about eleven o'clock and with a short stop to see the quaint town of Cricklade reached Lechlade easily about six. The canal after leaving Latton Locks where it is joined by the Wilts. and Berks. Canal is reedy and the tow paths are lined with bushes which makes towing no light matter. We stopped at the New Inn at Lechlade.'

1911

Perhaps the best-known quotation for the Thames & Severn is also the most evocative, of a journey of exploration into and through an enchanting landscape – romanticism at its best. In his *The Flower of Gloucester* published in 1911, E. Temple Thurston included one special statement, oft-quoted since:

'When you join the Thames and Severn Canal at Stroud, it is but twenty-eight miles and a few odd furlongs before you come to Inglesham, where the water of the canal joins the Isis and all signs of the tow-path are lost to you for ever. But those twenty-eight miles are worth a thousand for the wealth of their colour alone.'

Temple Thurston was especially fond of the Thames & Severn and lived for some years in Gloucestershire. However there are discrepancies in his account which suggest that, as he was a writer of fiction by profession (and a prolific one at that), this account too may be a combi-

Sapperton Tunnel has always attracted interest and a desire to see inside. About 1910-1912 Percy Melsome and his friend Wilfrid Compton, both from nearby Ewen, are about to enter the tunnel in their homemade boat by the light of a hurricane lamp. The Compton family were wheelwrights, undertakers and agricultural engineers in Ewen for several generations. Wilfrid died in 1977; Percy was lost in the First World War. (Photo courtesy Janet Compton, Cirencester)

nation of actual experiences along the midland canals linked via the workings of an observant and creative imagination into 'a clever interweaving of a series of different experiences', as the most recent published study concluded. However, none of that reduces the value of this book or of the vivid images created within its pages.

1916

Some pleasure traffic is recorded from the Minutes of meetings during the Gloucestershire County Council period of ownership (if only perhaps because they were part of talking-up the route for business as never before?) and the best-recorded of these is Peter Bonthron's journey in *My Holidays on Inland Waterways* in 1916. This writer covered 2,000 miles by motor boat through British waterways over a thirty-year period up to 1915, although actual dates are often not given. On one journey from Surrey via the Thames, the Thames & Severn was the first canal encountered on their trip into the midlands. At Inglesham a horse and horseman were hired to get them through the weeds all the way up to the tunnel. They had a break of journey at Cirencester due to the traditional Whitsun closure of the canal, and used the nearby railway station to escape and return a week later (there is almost a modern 'weekender' feel about their account). The summit proved to be 'not over-abundant' with water, the locks on the way down slow in filling, but their journey through the tunnel and descent into and through the Golden Valley was a remarkable experience. The journey from Cirencester to Wallbridge occupied one long day.

1933

William Bliss recorded his adventures by canoe in *Heart of England by waterway: a canoeing chronicle by river and canal.* He noted that it was necessary to cart one's canoe from Chalford to Cricklade.

Last but not least there are the fictional accounts where experiences of the Thames & Severn journey are included. Thomas Love Peacock has one description in *Crotchet Castle* (1924) but best known and most vivid is the passage of the Sapperton Tunnel in *Hornblower and the Atropos* (various editions inc. 1957 and 1965) by C.S. Forester (1899-1966) which describes the legging operation through the tunnel.

This iron girder bridge replaced an earlier structure across the Cirencester arm at Siddington for access to the village school c.1906. This view belongs to a few years later and is one of the few photographs taken on this section of canal. (Photo courtesy Corinium Museum Cirencester ref. 1977/200/70)

4 Restoration – The First Thirty Years 1972-2002

The walker along the towpath of the Thames & Severn in the summer of 2002 could enjoy some fifteen miles of right of way along the original line of the towpath plus another ten miles or so by using the Thames Path, designated as a National long-distance Trail in 1989, as an alternative footpath route for the eastern section of the canal's 'heritage line'. To that can be added the several options of paths through Hailey Wood in Cirencester Park which includes over two miles of the 'donkey path' above the tunnel from one entrance to the other. In the valley west of Chalford much of the towpath has remained in use on a regular basis since the closure of the canal in 1933, for access to places of employment as well as for recreational purposes, and – for the latter at least – it remains so. Elsewhere usage steadily grows as the charms of the route become better known and promoted. The accumulated achievement here is obvious – over 50% of the 'heritage' line of the Thames & Severn is now accessible on foot, and in almost equal distances on either side of the tunnel, providing one of the major restoration achievements in terms of accessibility. Walkers, cyclists and – in places – fishermen all make good use of this facility, which remains only one part of the overall restoration campaign.

As it celebrated its 30th anniversary in 2002, the Cotswold Canals Trust membership will have reviewed not only this particular achievement but progress made generally on all of its four main Aims. These were originally adopted in 1989 but were reshaped in the Trust's 25th anniversary year in 1997 as follows:

- to promote, for the benefit of the community, the re-opening of the Cotswold Canals (i.e. the Stroudwater and the Thames & Severn Canals)
- to promote the restoration of the two waterways to give a balance between the needs of navigation, development, recreation, heritage, landscape conservation, wildlife and natural habitats
- to promote the use of all the towpath as the Thames & Severn Way long distance footpath
- to achieve restoration of the Cotswold Canals as a navigable route from Saul Junction to the River Thames

Much effort has gone into all four of these Aims which, although they might be regarded by some as sequential activities, are by others (including the Trust) viewed essentially as work to be tackled in tandem. This brief summary can seek only to highlight some of the major achievements for this thirty-year period, considered at a time when the restoration programme seems set fair to take on a whole new level of activity and effort towards the final goal of through restoration to become part of the national network of leisure canals in Britain. As the opening chapter in this story, covering these first thirty years, comes to a close and another chapter begins, it is worth noting that the full story of restoring the Cotswold Canals (Stroudwater as well as Thames & Severn) will need to be written in due course, as is already being achieved for similar schemes elsewhere (see Further Reading).

This brief summary also limits itself to the Thames & Severn Canal, although of course much of the Trust's effort over thirty years has also been devoted to the Stroudwater as well. The marketing name of Cotswold Canals (adopted in 1990) seeks to unify all this activity along what is today essentially a single route, from Severn to Thames, albeit built originally in two stages by two groups of proprietors (with much overlap in personnel) and opened only ten years apart, in 1779 and 1789. The story for 1972-2002 is tackled here thematically rather than chronologically or topographically, although key work-sites and achievements on the ground are noted in the Guide section of this study as they are visited. Students of detail as well as timetable can do no better than consult the fine record built up in the pages of *The Trow*, the Trust's official magazine, which has been the point of reference for much of the information used in this study. Here can be found the round of activities, fundraising events, meetings, work parties, campaigns and crises large and small which are the lot of any amenity society seeking to convince the wider community of the merit of its aims and objectives.

A strong sense of nostalgia survived, and even perhaps continued to grow, for decades beyond the demise of the Thames & Severn and capitalising on it could well have been a useful starting point in the early 1970s. Such a romantic sense of loss can indeed be found in the writings of the principal canal authors, Tom Rolt perhaps expressing it most clearly in his classic book *Narrow Boat*, first published in November 1944. Discussing his feelings about 'indescribably forlorn' abandoned waterways, he found the Thames & Severn 'most beautiful and most tragic of all', not least because of the remarkable scenery through which it passed and the sense of time standing still, which of course many other writers before him had also experienced in the Cotswold landscape. Not surprisingly, when he wrote the short introduction to Espley & Duncan Young's guidebook in 1969 (itself a period piece now), he revisited this 'certain melancholy and nostalgic fascination' of canals long gone, although still felt that any restoration of the Thames & Severn (by which he also included the Stroudwater) to be 'extremely doubtful'. Other writers followed suit. Ronald Russell, author of *Lost Canals of England and Wales* (David & Charles, first published in 1971), produced a good summary of the state of the canal at that time, with a suitably nostalgic look over his shoulder too. So this 'most beautiful and most tragic' of canals seemed doomed to oblivion.

By contrast, a hard-headed realism was a hallmark of Humphrey Household's writings on this subject. Despite his love of this particular canal he could not escape the historical reality of its long – and ultimately unsuccessful – struggle to survive, and that view was also shared by Charles Hadfield. The latter wrote the brief but erudite introductions to each edition of Household's classic study (in 1969 and 1983), regretting in the first of these that the journey along the Thames & Severn was 'now impossible', although in the second welcoming the achievements to date and the continuing development of the restoration campaign. Household too was able to acknowledge the progress of restoration for his revised edition, remarking particularly on the achievement of restoring one of the tunnel portals.

However, the adrenaline and enthusiasm for canal restoration did not pass the Stroudwater and the Thames & Severn by. As elsewhere, a group of enthusiasts organised themselves and began the campaign, initially focussed upon the Stroudwater and the western end of the through line.

The early days of restoration; here the Priestman Cub dragline of the Stroudwater Canal Society is working along the Bowbridge to Griffin's Mill pound in the mid-1970s. (Photo courtesy Cotswold Canals Trust)

A preliminary meeting was called by a small committee led by Michael Ayland of Saul 'to examine the feasibility of restoring the Navigation from Framilode to Wallbridge, Stroud'. The room booked in Stroud Subscription Rooms for 12 May 1972 proved to be too small for the over 300 people who turned up and the main hall was used. So the Stroudwater Canal Society was formed in December of that year. Its six Aims make interesting reading when compared to those later adopted in various forms by the successor Trust. Amongst its plans were:

- to encourage the amenity use of the Stroudwater and the Thames & Severn Canals for boating, walking, fishing and other recreational pursuits
- to promote an active interest in all aspects of the waterway
- to prevent any further deterioration in the canals which could impede ultimate complete restoration
- to assist the local authority in including the canal in its plans for amenity improvement in the Stroud valleys

There is a clear emphasis on amenity benefit and the need to preserve and interpret the heritage value of the canal line, as pre-requisites for any restoration attempt. By so doing, the new Society was seeking to give support to the pioneering work done by Gloucestershire County Council as planning authority (as well of course as principal landowner) in its own work, such as the Stroud Valleys Facelift project of which the major enhancement remains the area around Chalford Wharf. Restoration as a specific aim in itself achieved a more focussed priority status as the Society grew, as its ability to prevent further deterioration was recognised, and as it gained political support for this ultimate objective.

Once formed, it was natural for the new Society to set about some physical work on the ground. Volunteers appeared and projects were proposed, and this pattern has continued in a more or less continuous process ever since, recognising throughout the constant pressure to attract and retain sufficient volunteers for physical activity. Indeed some of the inevitable growing pains and tensions of the early years within the organisation related directly to the key issue as to what were the real priorities. Was digging out the infilled canal and repairing locks along available stretches as important as trying to safeguard the whole length from further degradation? How important was it to have overall polices which other public bodies could address and – hopefully – support? How high a campaigning profile should the new body have? Should it be radical and interventionist and/or be supportive of the (apparently) slower-moving strategies of the various public bodies? Indeed, are any or all of these issues necessarily in conflict with each other or could they be tackled together? These were all questions much debated, especially in view of the limited resources of funding and manpower, and in each case there was a resolution, and an example of a turning point, where a victory achieved had much wider implications in the longer term.

Looking back over thirty years, *The Trow* produced its own summary of the 'work on the ground' element of these choices for action, where the Trust took a lead, listing eighteen

Restoration work in progress on the Coates portal c.1976/1977. (Photo courtesy Chris Bowler, Cirencester)

Stonemason Bruce Russell of Tetbury putting the finishing touches to the detailing of the Coates portal, c.*1976/1977.* (Photo courtesy Chris Bowler, Cirencester)

successful projects from west to east. This is not comprehensive but does capture the flavour of the story (dates do not necessarily reflect continuous activity nor include ongoing maintenance work):

Wallbridge: dredged by contractors to original profile; spoil transferred and landscaped on former Stroud Brewery site by volunteers (1990/1996/1998)

Wallbridge Upper Lock: excavated (1988), repaired by Stroud Valleys Project (1989-1990) and re-gated by the Trust (1992-1994)

Bowbridge: the Trust's first work site. A ¾-mile pound dredged using Trust-owned equipment, and re-flooded (1972-1975)

Griffins Mill Lock: structural repairs and one top gate constructed (1975-1976) plus work on pound up to *Ham Mill Lock* (1976-1980)

Jubilee Bridge: repaired and refurbished (1976/1988/1998 and 2002)

Bagpath Bridge: repairs to the parapet (1978-1979)

Daneway Portal: clearance of approach and wall repairs (1981-1982) and major repairs to western portal of Sapperton Tunnel (project 1993-1996, work on structure 1996)

A working party engaged on tidying up and landscaping around the restored Coates portal soon after the unveiling of this major conservation project in 1977. (Photo Robert Carr, Dursley, courtesy Cotswold Canals Trust)

Coates Portal: restoration of the eastern portal (1976, completed 1978), with clearance of King's Reach and pound to roundhouse etc (1975-1979, 1995-1996)

Halfway Bridge: major repairs to 'a rare example of a T&SC stone bridge' (1997-1998)

Park Leaze: footpath clearance of new permissive right of way (1995-1996)

Siddington Locks: major landscaping project with minor structural works, noted as 'a real credit to the Trust' (1992 onwards), and re-opening of Siddington to Eisey towpath (1993 but begun along the eastern section in 1978)

Claymeadow Cutting: dredging to original profile, tree management and towpath surfacing works (1995-1999)

Northmoor Pound: towpath and canal bed clearance work (1994 onwards)

Boxwell Spring Lock: compete rebuild of nearside wall, offside structural repairs and associated landscaping (1992-1995)

Wilmoreway Lower Lock: rebuilding of offside wall, major works on bridge, structural works on side pond, work on pounds above and below and associated landscaping of the area (1980, 1995-1998)

Wilmoreway Lock with derelict cottage and bridge in March 1981, making a sharp contrast with the scene today, with lock and bridge rebuilt. Only the cottage remains derelict. (Photo Peter Chadwick, Swindon, courtesy Cotswold Canals Trust)

Spine Road Pound: profiling works on both sides of the Spine Road (1995 onwards)

Cerney Wick Lock: towpath work (1978 onwards), brickwork repairs (1982-1986) and installation of top gates (1990)

Latton Culvert: major culvert under new Latton by-pass, a ten-year campaign concluding with construction in 1997

A further twelve significant projects were listed along the Stroudwater, which includes the substantial rebuilding work at the Eastington, Blunder and Newtown group of locks, itself an excellent example of reconstruction paying dividends in terms of overall regeneration; plus Ryford double lock and various key bridge sites along the seven mile length.

This is a formidable list, for an essentially voluntary organisation reliant upon a relatively small scale of voluntary effort for nearly all its work, plus externally funded schemes of one kind or another as various national initiatives created opportunities. It is significant that an early campaign was the programme of dredging the pound between Bowbridge and Griffin's Mill, with work on the locks at either end. Here were learnt the advantages and disadvantages of acquiring and maintaining plant and equipment for the purpose, of trying to maintain a programme over more than a limited period using a small team of volunteers, and of negotiating a host of liaison issues with neighbouring landowners. To walk this section today, and to see it in water, is to appreciate the amenity value years later of making changes on the ground,

Working parties dividing up the tasks in the canal bed above the lock at Bowbridge, another view of the early years of the Trust's activities. (Photo courtesy Cotswold Canals Trust)

which is itself one of the most powerful arguments for active physical intervention. Those arguments are too well rehearsed in the waterways literature to need repetition here.

By the time the Stroudwater Canal Society had transformed itself into the Stroudwater, Thames & Severn Canal Trust Ltd in April 1975, an eastern end branch had been formed and a reasonable balance of activity could be inspected along much of the 'heritage line'. One of the key issues since 1972 has been tackling the relative scale of loss of access when comparing the 7½ miles of towpath up from Stroud as far as the west of the tunnel and the 18-plus miles from the tunnel eastwards to the Thames. In general terms much of the western section remained (and remains) in local authority ownership, with an accessible towpath, whereas much of the eastern section was sold off and indeed divided up between neighbouring landowners. The records show a substantial programme of such selling off immediately after the closure decision had been implemented for the canal east of Whitehall Bridge at the end of January 1927. Not unnaturally, some considerable lengths of the most easterly sections from Cricklade have long since reverted to agricultural land with the canal bed infilled and the towpath obliterated. So the challenges to the Trust were differently balanced to west and east.

The work at and around Wilmoreway Locks makes a similar impact in terms of environmental improvement as achieved along some of the western sections in the Frome valley. Dredging of the canal bed and work on the lock and the bridge alongside have together achieved a group effect, which can also be seen at nearby Cerney Wick Lock. Indeed the opening up of the whole line as a through footpath route from Siddington to Latton provides a backbone for such activity and access. To the visitor, the ability to infill – and sustain – sections of the canal with water is a key indication of success (the Bowbridge project is again the obvious example), plus the repair or renewal of the principal structures such as locks. Here there is a detailed study to be made on the structural requirements and heritage merit of each individual structure, tailored always to the knowledge that this was a working waterway with running repairs (make do and mend) – as well as the occasional major rebuilding – as key features of its history. It can be assumed that none of the locks survive as intact and unaltered heritage structures from the 1780s, although some come close; all will have been repaired, altered or amended in some way, but without a doubt they represent a key part of the overall historical value of the Thames & Severn, special to this canal and to no other.

Right at the start of the canal in Stroud, Wallbridge Upper Lock looks better than it has done for years, with the removal of the 'rubbish dump' it had become and the installation of new lock gates. One gate for Griffin's Mill Lock was constructed on behalf of the Trust as an early project but its installation in 1975 was short-lived, and so the hanging of the top gates at Cerney Wick in 1990 proved to be the first set of new gates to be installed along the entire length of the Thames & Severn since closure. As at Wilmoreway, significant rebuilding also took place at Boxwell Spring Lock, whereas the Siddington group was the subject of a care and maintenance approach.

The bridges of the Stroudwater and the Thames & Severn Canal provide another fascinating study. Some are entirely in stone, of which Red Lion and Tarlton Road are perhaps the best examples, dating respectively from 1785 and 1823. Others are a mixture of stone and brick, which is one of the reasons why Trewsbury Bridge is special, in rough mortared stone with a minimum of brick repairs. Most have stone copings and sometimes stone abutments to an otherwise brick bridge, and the elegant shape of many of these bridges – in brick as well as in stone – is another significant heritage feature of the Thames & Severn. It is a pity that the dry stone bridges, such as the example at Eisey, no longer survive. The records seem to show that they were built in small groups as part of contracts for work, so that the style might vary slightly between one team and another, bearing in mind that this work was not necessarily sequential or systematic from west to east. The walk up from Stanton's Bridge (itself repaired) to Brimscombe reveals a fine group, including the repaired Bagpath Bridge, and there are equally interesting examples scattered along the eastern sections, notably the rebuilt Halfway, Siddington, Cowground and not least Oatlands Bridge, isolated in the fields near Kempsford. Nearby Inglesham, although *private*, is a delightful humpback over the canal.

Sapperton Tunnel is without doubt the most significant single structure along the canal line and the restoration of the two portals, the eastern in 1976-1978 and the western in 1996, made a significant impact upon public appreciation of the value of the canal in historical, architectural and conservation terms. Much support was gathered, particularly because interest in the canal's architecture is widespread (and not always confined to supporters of canal restoration either), and also perhaps because these two portals – although they remain in the private ownership of the Bathurst Estate – provide easy access to this architectural heritage in a way in which other buildings connected with the canal cannot do. The rehabilitation of a number of canal buildings, including several of the roundhouses, as private homes over the past two decades or so is good news in one sense, but a lessening of public access, except at a distance, is another issue. It is important that the remaining unrestored and architecturally significant buildings along the line of both Stroudwater and Thames & Severn canals should be included within the overall restoration campaign to provide both accessibility and interpretation in the future. This and the creation of an overall environmental strategy for all aspects of the natural history of the canals, which this Guide does not seek to cover, will be important yardsticks for success.

None of the practical work on the ground could have achieved its proper impact without the development of long-term strategies to provide a framework for action, with of course the accompanying political pressure. Such strategies have evolved over time, but have nevertheless built into a solid body of accumulating information and guidance. A summary list of the key publications is included here. Right from the outset an initial feasibility study for the seven miles of the Stroudwater up to Stroud formed part of the campaign in 1972, but without doubt the greatest impact in the early days was made by the Freeman Fox & Partners report of 1976 which covered the entire line from Severn to Thames, estimating a restoration cost of some £8 million and a programme of work over some twenty years. This price tag was the key issue for debate for – probably – the next decade, together with a growing appreciation that here was a realisable project, given support and funding.

The raft of reports produced in the 1990s took the campaign into an altogether more political forum. Local Plans of the relevant local authorities began to introduce supportive statements seeking to protect the line of the canal against further encroachment (Cotswold and Stroud district councils in particular), and the designation of conservation area status had a major impact in asserting such protection. The Stroud Industrial Heritage Conservation Area (first designated in 1987) protected a considerable length and Cotswold District Council followed with similar and contiguous designations on either side of Sapperton Tunnel. In the eastern section, the Upper Thames Plan provides similar designation.

Reports from consulting engineers W.S. Atkins in 1991 and 1994 and Sir William Halcrow & Partners in 1991 and 1996 provided solid feasibility studies for the engineering issues on different sections, leading to the Cotswold Canals Corridor Study in April 1996 which produced a strategy for the development and management of the entire canal route. The funding and subsequent adoption of this Study by the relevant local authorities was another turning point, with obvious long-term implications. In 1998, the Inland Waterways Amenity Advisory Council (IWAAC) published an analysis into national waterway restoration schemes; it proposed the Stroudwater amongst the twenty-one schemes in the priority category (recommending immediate funding), with the Thames & Severn in the second category for funding on a five to ten year timescale.

Government initiatives in 1999 and 2000 to support waterway restoration then provided the opportunity for the Cotswold Canals scheme to campaign for and achieve priority in the national bidding list. With partnership as the key, the Cotswold Canals Partnership was formed in July 2001 at the launch of the latest feasibility study by British Waterways, pulling together the work of earlier years, and estimating restoration costs at some £82 million. It is that Partnership which now seeks to implement the restoration proposals, mandated by a strong representation of not only British Waterways and The Waterways Trust but the regional development agency, the Environment Agency, the two county councils and three district councils through whose areas the canals run, the Cotswold Canals Trust and other bodies. It is the detailed work undertaken by this body which will determine the success or failure in the twenty-first century of the 'great undertaking' bringing back to life the achievement of its eighteenth-century predecessors.

All of the projects listed above represent achievements along the way in the campaign for conservation and restoration. Two in particular should also be noted, both long, complicated, determined and (inevitably) exhausting campaigns to prevent a break in the line and therefore a loss of both purpose and momentum. Both were stimulated by road schemes, the first the east-west by-pass in Stroud in the 1970s-1980s and the second the Latton by-pass over a ten-year period up to 1997. In Stroud, several routes were proposed for a new inner ring road, two of which would have removed the canal completely through its Wallbridge section. After a battle, the route finally chosen and built – and now Dr Newton's Way – severed a short section of the canal's 'heritage line' beneath the railway viaduct but protected its route underneath the new road.

Latton was an altogether more costly threat, initially threatening to sever the line, and later in the demand for full costs to install a culvert to protect the line, awaiting future restoration. This battle was of national significance, and the victory was reflected in new government guidelines issued in July 2001 requiring the Highways Agency to take waterway restoration into account when planning new roads or making improvements and to provide suitable culverts where appropriate. Other waterway campaigns had helped this cause, but future travellers making use of the Latton culvert can reflect upon the especial significance of this structure in the overall programme of restoration of the Cotswold Canals in its first thirty years between 1972-2002.

Key Reports
1972 *The Thames & Severn Waterway Link: Part One – The Stroudwater Canal.*

1976 *Stroudwater Navigation and Thames & Seven Canal: Preliminary engineering report on the feasibility of restoring the canal to through navigation* by Freeman Fox Braine & Partners.

1991 *Saul Junction to Ocean Railway Bridge* by W.S. Atkins & Partners.

1991 *Inglesham to Cotswold Water Park* by Sir William Halcrow & Partners.

1993 *Golden Valley Survey* by Gloucestershire Wildlife Trust.

1994 *Ocean Railway Bridge to Sapperton tunnel* by W.S. Atkins & Partners.

1996 *Cotswold Water Park to Sapperton Tunnel* by Sir William Halcrow & Partners.

1996 *Cotswold Canals Corridor Study* by Waterway Environment Services.

1998 *Waterway Restoration Priorities* (IWAAC).

1999 *WildWorks* – Biodiversity Survey and Recommendations for proposed restoration, Spine Road to Latton Junction

2000 *Waterways for Tomorrow* - Government Vision for Inland Waterways (DETR).

2001 *Report into the Feasibility of Restoring the Cotswold Canals* for The Waterways Trust.

changeover from right to left-hand side. All this has gone, leaving only a footpath (keep straight ahead just beyond the viaduct) which soon reaches the point where the line of the canal has been truncated – a pleasant surprise with a small picnic area where it is difficult to appreciate that this is only half a mile from the centre of Stroud.

New housing on the left covers the site of Arundel's Mill which is typical of the many mill-sites to be encountered along the valley floor up to and beyond Chalford. As here, many were named after one of the principal owners in their history; Richard Arundel owned this mill in the early seventeenth century. It was equally typical for the many variations in its use, usually based upon the processing of wool. Products here included the manufacture of artificial manure during the nineteenth century and a dyeing business survived as its last use. The site is now indicated by its dredged mill-pond and sluices. On the opposite bank stood Capel's Mill, where cloth and shoddy were produced. Both made use of the considerable power to be obtained from the nearby River Frome which is culverted under the canal at this point. With the mills eventually turning to steam power, they became large customers of the canal carriers for their supplies of coal.

Despite all the changes, this valley floor of the Frome represents a remarkable surviving landscape of industrial history. Many of the earlier stone mill buildings may have been replaced, their modern successors more functional than aesthetic, but the towpath walk is an excellent way to appreciate the grouping of buildings, the relationship of the canal to them, and – equally intriguing – the points of access via old tracks and paths down into and across the valley floor from the cottages and communities on the hillsides around. This is how many of the mill workers got to their work, and the fine group of canal accommodation bridges along the whole section up to Chalford and beyond remain as evidence of the community history in the valleys; many are still well used today and form a network of leisure footpaths. Equally, it can be appreciated how relatively easy was the supply of coal from the canalside into the mill, loading directly from the barge tied up to a small wharf. Just up the valley side to the right, the Gloucester-Stroud-Swindon railway line makes its own long climb up the valley to cross the hills via its own tunnel at Sapperton. The story of this line is all part of the early history of the Great Western Railway in this area, which included the much-used and fondly-recalled local services with frequent – and tiny – halts between Stroud and Chalford.

Approaching Bowbridge Lock the towpath becomes a well-worn single-width path in the narrow confine between the River Frome and the canal, only yards apart here. Steps up and over the road lead to the lock. Here is another example of a north-south route, originally a pack-horse route no doubt, crossing the valley. Before the turnpike road was built along the Frome valley in 1814 (the present road) most tracks kept to the higher ground on both sides of the valley and may still be traced as lanes. Bowbridge is the site of the first real achievement in restoration by the Cotswold Canals Trust. Work began on this section in 1972 and continued eastwards in various stages for some eight years. A strong dam has been built across the lock in the position of the upper gates and this holds back the correct depth of water in a section that has effectively been returned to navigable condition. When in water, this area cannot fail to make the point that restoration can enhance the environment, with an especially fine view up to Stanton's Bridge. Also restored was the circular overflow weir just above the lock (now protected with a grille), and similar to others on the Stroudwater Canal at Ebley and Eastington. There is also stone edging to the towpath just above the lock which

Stanton's Bridge in the Frome valley, between Bowbridge and Griffin's Mill locks, a classic canal scene, photographed here in 1955 and restored and re-watered as an early project of the Canal Trust in the 1970s. (Photo Frank Lloyd, courtesy & copyright British Waterways Archives, Gloucester, ref. 5269)

enabled barges to tie up and unload coal etc. directly into the dye-works alongside. The dye-house is all that survives of the Bowbridge mills group.

Here too is the first of the surviving Thames & Severn Canal milestones which recorded the distance every half-mile from Wallbridge at the Stroud end and Inglesham Junction on the Thames. This information was required for the benefit of canal users who paid tolls for their passage of the canal both by weight and by distance (see pp.68-69 for the story of the canal's milestones). The Bowbridge stone (*Walbridge 1*) was well sited to be used as a mooring post for the wharf here and was not the only one used in this way.

Bowbridge to Brimscombe

The housing development of Bowbridge Lock immediately adjoins the canal for the next section, and the restored waterway continues under Stanton's Bridge and up almost to Griffin's Lock. This was dredged during 1975 when repairs were also made to the bridge. This and other stretches of water are now fished by local angling clubs. The towpath is well used and is pleasant easy walking, becoming even more rural in outlook. A great deal of major clearance work and dredging was carried out at Griffin's Lock and on towards Ham Mill Lock by the Trust during 1975-1976, even to the extent of making a new top lock gate. Although the lock remains derelict, at least further deterioration has been arrested; a concrete block weir is now built across the top gate position in an attempt to retain water in the section up to Ham Mill Lock and so restrict the growth of weeds in the canal. Apart from creating the visual attractiveness of a re-watered section compared with other dry and neglected areas further on, such relatively simple and cost-effective measures have a beneficial effect upon the otherwise uncontrolled flow of water through derelict locks and thus ensure a measure of conservation of deteriorating brickwork.

With its mast down, this barge (perhaps a trow?) is tied up at Bowbridge 'upper wharf' just above the lock, with Stafford's Mill in the background. Date unknown but perhaps c.1930. (Copies of this photograph are in Gloucestershire Records Office ref. GPS 320/132 and Corinium Museum Cirencester ref. 1977/259/6)

Above Griffin's Lock is Jubilee Bridge, a delightful small iron latticework footbridge. This is another example of serving the needs of the local community, in this case particularly workers to and from Griffin's Mill. The name of the bridge is a clue to its dating; it is believed to have been built at the time of the Golden or Diamond Jubilees of Queen Victoria in 1887 or 1897 (although Household dates it to 1903). It replaced a temporary bridge which had been built in 1842 to restore the right of way after the collapse of the original bridge through neglect. Jubilee Bridge has itself been restored and was recently repainted at the time of this survey.

Modern industrial uses in the mill buildings and mill sites have been far more varied than the earlier reliance upon the woollen trade in all its forms, uses ranging from the production of powered invalid cars to high-tech equipment. For example, at Griffin's Mill a late nine-teenth-century three-storeyed building stands on the site of a sixteenth-century mill; a woollen mill until 1838, it was converted into a timber and saw mill. It was also typical in that it was utilised for the production of wooden parts for aircraft during the two world wars. Here too is another small wharf, edged with stone blocks, for the unloading of coal into the mill. Along this section can be found a milestone (*Walbridge 1½*).

The canal then proceeds in a straight line towards Ham Mill Lock and Bridge, again taking its name from the adjacent mill, which again is on a sixteenth-century site. Much enlarged at various stages in the nineteenth century, when a good many of the Stroud textile mills were modernised or completely rebuilt, it survived as a woollen mill until 1899. What remains is a good example of its type, complete with a tapering stone chimney. At the time of survey it

1. *Thames barge, bow-hauled by two men, rounding the bend approaching Daneway portal in 1793; the tunnel cottage is in the background. This vessel was one of the company's improved design, made at its Bourne yards.* (Illustration courtesy National Waterways Museum, Gloucester)

2. *A Thames barge emerges from Sapperton tunnel in 1790, its mast being raised to continue the journey. The New Inn (later Tunnel House) is on the bank behind.* (Illustration courtesy National Waterways Museum, Gloucester)

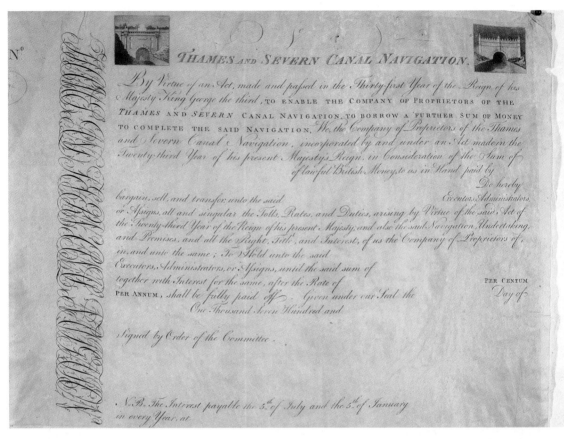

THAMES AND SEVERN CANAL NAVIGATION.

By Virtue of an Act, made and passed in the Thirty-first Year of the Reign of his Majesty King George the third, TO ENABLE THE COMPANY OF PROPRIETORS OF THE THAMES AND SEVERN CANAL NAVIGATION, TO BORROW A FURTHER SUM OF MONEY TO COMPLETE THE SAID NAVIGATION, *We, the Company of Proprietors of the Thames and Severn Canal Navigation, incorporated by and under an Act made in the Twenty-third Year of his present Majesty's Reign, in Consideration of the Sum of*

of lawful British Money, to us in Hand paid by Do hereby

bargain, sell, and transfer unto the said Executors, Administrators, *or Assigns, all and singular the Tolls, Rates, and Duties, arising by Virtue of the said Act of the Twenty-third Year of the Reign of his present Majesty; and also the said Navigation, Undertaking, and Premises, and all the Right, Title, and Interest, of us the Company of Proprietors of, in, and unto the same; To Hold unto the said Executors, Administrators, or Assigns, until the said sum of together with Interest for the same, after the Rate of*

PER CENTUM

PER ANNUM, *shall be fully paid off. Given under our Seal the* Day of

One Thousand Seven Hundred and

Signed by Order of the Committee.

N.B. The Interest payable the 5th of July and the 5th of January in every Year, at

3. *Second issue (1791) share certificate of the Thames & Severn Canal Navigation. The coloured vignettes show both tunnel portals clearly, as symbols of the enterprise.* (Illustration courtesy National Waterways Museum, Gloucester)

4. *The Golden Valley richly deserves its name in this 1960s view of Chalford roundhouse and Chalford Place behind.*

5. This view of Inglesham roundhouse, lock and bridge was published on 1 June 1793 by J. & J. Boydell of London. A barge mast can be seen downriver in Lechlade and the representation of the canal features shows how they looked in the very early years of the canal's life.

6. Lechlade coal wharf, from a newly rediscovered painting of 1859 by Louisa Wheeler, the twenty-six-year-old daughter of a Lechlade blacksmith. Ha'penny Bridge is on the right. (Illustration courtesy Lechlade Historical Society)

7. *The Wallbridge wharf of the Thames &
Severn Canal, with the company's warehouse
on the right in this view on 14 May 1980; the
railway bridge across the Upper Lock can also
be seen.* (Photo author)

8. *Jubilee Bridge on 28 March 1985, looking
across the canal to Griffin's mill buildings – a
classic Frome valley view with industrial
buildings and canal close together.*
(Photo author)

9. Very last days for the Canal Company's warehouse and office building at Brimscombe Port, seen here on 16 April 1965, only a short time before demolition began.

10. Canal Cottage to the left, Wharf House in the centre and the salt warehouse on the right – the three surviving canal buildings at Brimscombe Port in the 1980s. Only the salt warehouse survives today. (Photo courtesy Theo Stening, Tetbury)

11. *The advertising for James Smart's business at Chalford wharf still survives on the gable end of his house in May 2000.* (Photo author)

12. *Early autumn scene in 1976 at Puck Mill with the old Oak Inn on the right.* (Photo courtesy Cotswold Canals Trust)

13 & 14. *The bridges of the Thames & Severn are one of its characteristic features, none more so than Whitehall Bridge, isolated in the Golden Valley and a delightful spot to visit. Its datestone WD 1784 recalls William Dennis who built it. It was Whitehall Bridge which was the cut-off point when the canal was closed to the east of here in 1927. Photographed on 14 July 2002.* (Photos author)

Above: 15. *Tunnel cottage at Daneway recorded here on 18 April 1964 at a time when any restoration of the canal must have seemed a forlorn dream.*

Opposite: *16. Daneway, exactly twenty years later on 20 April 1984, with the portal in dereliction but some work achieved in conserving the walls of the canal bed.* (Photo author).

17. The Daneway portal restored, seen here on 21 September 1996. (Photo Maureen Poulton, courtesy Cotswold Canals Trust)

18. *Another familiar scene for many decades, the derelict Coates portal, deep in beech mast on 21 November 1964. Ivy growth caused a steady deterioration in the façade over the years.*

19. *The Earl Bathurst performing the unveiling of the restored Coates portal on 23 July 1977.* (Photo author)

20. *Stone mason Bruce Russell puts the finishing touches to his handiwork on the Coates portal in 1978.* (Photo courtesy Cotswold Canals Trust)

21. *Wilmoreway Lower Lock and Bridge on 19 July 2002, one of the obvious beneficial outcomes of restoration activity during the 1990s.* (Photo author)

22. The restoration worksite at Cerney Wick Lock on 14 April 1984. The appeal for volunteers was an ever-present feature. (Photo author)

23. Arguably one of the most attractive sights on the whole canal – the restored upper lock and roundhouse at Cerney Wick, photographed here in March 2000. (Photo author)

24 & 25. *Marston Meysey roundhouse stood empty and forlorn for some years before its deterioration was taken in hand. These two views, taken over fifteen years apart, show that process. Today it has been preserved and rehabilitated as part of a modern house. 1972 and 15 June 1986.* (Photos author)

26. *Splendid example of the Thames &
Severn series of milestones, this one
complete with plate at Inglesham in July
2002. This is the final stone in the
sequence from Walbridge in Stroud.*
(Photo author)

27. *The Latton culvert is installed, as
the road works proceed all around, 8
August 1997.* (Photo Keith
Harding, courtesy Cotswold Canals
Trust)

28. Oatlands bridge alone in the fields near Kempsford, 1997. (Photo courtesy Theo Stening, Tetbury)

29. Landscaping on a grand scale – these stands of beech trees on the skyline above Sapperton Tunnel each mark a spoil tip from the period of tunnel construction. Seen from the west, autumn 1997. (Photo courtesy Theo Stening, Tetbury)

30 & 31. The section between the locks at Bowbridge and Griffin's Mill remains one of the areas of greatest effort and achievement by Trust volunteers in the past thirty years. The pound is now back in water and the rebuilding of Stanton's Bridge, a charming brick bridge and a good example of an accommodation bridge across the canal, has added to its appeal as well as its heritage value. These two views support that view: in the earlier photograph – sometime in the mid-1970s – the dragline is at work and the bridge awaits repair. In the later view on 10 June 2002, the results can be fully appreciated. (Photos author)

was empty, having been occupied until recently by Carpets of Worth and thus retaining some small link with its old 'woollen' days. An interesting historical point is that the last working barge load of coal on the Thames & Severn Canal was brought up here from the west to Ham Mill in 1933 in the barge *Dorothy* owned by E.T. Ward & Sons Ltd, carriers of Stroud. The barge tied up just above the lock and was unloaded straight into the mill. Now there is a concrete block weir built across the position of the top gates and deeply-worn tow-rope grooves can be seen cut into the underside of the arch of the bridge. A recent rediscovery during clearance works is an impressive spill-weir alongside this lock.

Not far along is Bagpath Bridge (also called Phoenix Bridge), another fine example and extensively rebuilt by a small team of Trust members with new work on the parapets and abutments in 1978-1979. This gave access across the canal to the former Thrupp Mill. It was in a foundry established on this site in the 1830s – the Phoenix Iron Works – that John Ferrabee established a reputation for the manufacture of textile machinery and lawn mowers, an early example of which is preserved and displayed in the recently-opened Museum in the Park in Stroud. Modern factory buildings now cover the site.

Not apparent down on the cut but very obvious when viewed from Rodborough Common high above, the line of the canal is all the while curving gently in an arc from south to east, as it follows the Frome valley. This can be detected in the next section towards Brimscombe, which also includes another fine example of a milestone (*Walbridge 2*). This is sited just before the infilling starts at the approach to Hope Mill Lock (also called Ridler's

Edwin Clark & Co's Canal Ironworks boat-building yard at Hope Mills near Brimscombe c.1889. The company operated a flourishing business here until the death of its founder in 1896. His home, Hope Villa, is in the background (photo courtesy Corinium Museum Cirencester ref. 1988/164/1)

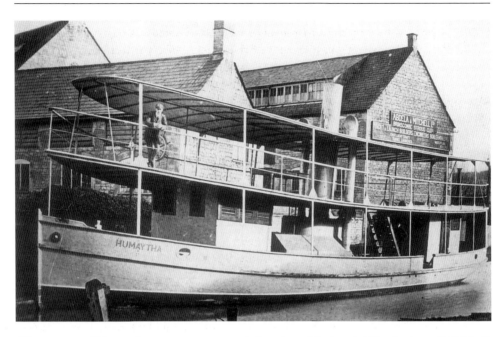

The steam vessel Humaytha *represents a very typical product of the boat-building business of Abdela & Mitchell Ltd at Hope Mills, Brimscombe. Designed and constructed in 1905 for use in Brazil, it had a gross tonnage of 27 tons, was 75ft long, with a 150hp engine, making it ideal for use along South American or other colonial river systems.* (Photo courtesy Stan Gardiner Collection)

Lock), one of the more obvious blockages to reconstructing the canal's original line. On the left, the surviving buildings of Hope Mill, largely rebuilt early in the nineteenth century, were used as a silk mill and are thought to be the last of this type of mill to operate in the Stroud valley. On the right, still nicely labelled 'Canal Ironworks Brimscombe', is a group of industrial buildings occupied by various companies, including Air Plants Ltd., actually on the canal line. This is the site of an enterprising private boat building yard which grew up and thrived for many years. It was initially set up by Edwin Clark & Co. in 1878 but was later taken over by Abdela & Mitchell Ltd., in 1899. There is some continuity here, for the present occupiers are themselves a successor company.

All types of boats were built ranging from small sailing boats to large steam screw and paddle river launches, many for use in South America. The yard continued building until 1934, using the canal to get its boats out, but following the official abandonment of the canal in 1933 it became necessary to use road transport, with boats often in pieces for assembly elsewhere, and the yard finally ceased activity just prior to the Second World War. The yard had both open and covered slipways launching its boats at an angle into the canal just above the lock; the old mill buildings on the towpath side of the canal were used as offices and as the boiler and engine factory. An excellent photographic record exists of most of the craft built there and of the yard, the building and the workforce (see Further Reading). Several of the vessels built at this yard are known to survive in various countries. The old boat-building sheds angled to the canal and a long line of open sheds at the rear have all now been replaced by modern buildings.

The towpath, without much accompanying canal, follows round to Gough's Orchard Lock and Bridge just alongside the once-extensive Brimscombe Mills. The lock has been known by several names locally, reflecting the owners and lessees of the mill buildings; Dallaway's recalls the family who occupied the site at the time the canal was constructed; Lewis the subsequent miller, and Evans from the well-established firm of P.C. Evans & Sons which had 124 looms at work there in 1889. Subsequent amalgamations led to closure and eventually to demolition and only part of the mill now remains. Of the lock itself, partial infilling is rather unsightly and from here the canal has been infilled and levelled up. However, its line remains clear, especially at the approach to the Ship Inn at Brimscombe, its painted sign showing its associations with the canal and this is the first genuine canalside public house since leaving Stroud, 2½ miles away. Together with two other public houses now closed – the Nelson and the Port – it served the needs of the employees at the Port and the boatmen who were held up there for the loading and unloading of cargoes.

Nothing remains of the substantial Brimscombe Bridge which once spanned the canal and allowed the towpath to change sides for the approach to the Port. Indeed the old line here takes some working out; road improvements have re-landscaped Brimscombe Corner and the River Frome has also been re-aligned. Directly ahead, the curving line of the access road to and past the modern factory buildings follows the canal line, and leads to a range of earlier

A remarkable surviving scene of a working boat on the Thames & Severn; coal is being unloaded from the longboat Alert *owned by A.M. Pearce of Brimscombe into Brimscombe Mills, undated but probably between 1910-1930. The boat is moored by the stern to the top gates of Gough's Orchard Lock and the coal is being unloaded straight into the mill by two men (unrelated) by the name of Davis, of Chalford. Much of this mill has now gone.* (Photo courtesy Stan Gardiner Collection, original Miss Florrie Davis, Chalford)

Milestones

Carriage of goods on the canal system was chargeable by tonnage and distance carried, a sender paying freight to the carrier and toll to the canal company. So information on the length of any given journey was important in the successful management of the system. Canal acts required mileposts to be fixed on the banks so that tolls could be calculated. Hence the milestones with their cast iron plates could be found at half-mile intervals along the whole length of the Thames & Severn, except on the Cirencester arm and through or over the top of Sapperton Tunnel. This is a total of fifty-two stones, not all of which survive of course. The location of some twenty accessible stones is recorded in this survey as at July 2002, but there are only four accessible, albeit re-sited, mileplates – at Chalford Wharf, Brimscombe Port and Eisey Manor Farm – an indication of the effect of theft and loss over the years. Restoration of the Cotswold Canals should include rehabilitation of this important part of the story, including the provision of a new series of plates.

Not a great deal is known about the history of the Thames & Severn set of stones and plates, except that they are a uniform group and appear to belong to one period and one installation. Eighteenth-century mileposts were often of wood or stone; in the early nineteenth century cast-iron mileposts became common, of which there are many examples still to be found along the canal system. The Act of 1783 authorising the canal's construction required 'stones to be erected every half mile', for which the detailed wording (Clause XCI) required 'that as soon as conveniently may be, after the said Canal and Collateral Cut shall be completed, the said Company of Proprietors shall cause the same to be measured, and Stones to be erected, and for ever after maintained, on the side or sides thereof, at the distance of half a mile from each other'. From this it can be assumed that the Thames & Severn set belongs to the early years of the canal's construction, probably from the outset in the late 1780s.

Stones and plates appear to be part of a contemporary installation. Each plate reads on the mile and the half-mile from Wallbridge, so that the measurements from Inglesham are to the quarter-mile and three-quarter mile. Hence the plate at Chalford reads *Walbridge 4 Inglesham 24 ¼*, with only one l in the spelling of Wallbridge, the place name in Stroud which otherwise has a double l. Without doubt these plates were locally made, and the stones were also sourced from local material, probably as a single contract. Interestingly, there are two types of stone, a flat-topped and a rather more attractive round-headed stone, in each case mirroring the contemporary fashion of milestones on the turnpike road system. It would be fascinating to know more about who made these stones and plates and when.

Whilst many plates remain unaccounted for (presumed stolen – at least one has disappeared since the Towpath Guide was published in 1984), a number have been rescued over the years and include some replica plates which have themselves become part of the overall collection. The Trust has the original *Walbridge 7 ½* in its archive. Museums in the county have a total of fourteen original and replica plates. The National Waterways Museum in Gloucester has an original *Walbridge 28* on display and another *Walbridge 5 ½* recently added from the late Harry Townley's collection. The Corinium Museum in Cirencester has an original *Walbridge 26 ½* and a replica *Walbridge 5 ½* plate, plus the complete stone with *Walbridge 16* plate intact from the towpath near Cowground Bridge at Siddington, donated by the landowner in 1971. The Museum in the Park collection in Stroud include those formerly in the late W.E. Duncan Young's Roundhouse Museum in Chalford; there are eight, some originals and some replicas: *Walbridge 2* (two), *Walbridge 2 ½* (two), *Walbridge 4 ½*, *Walbridge 5*, *Walbridge 10* and *Walbridge 15*. In the Folk Museum in Westgate in Gloucester is an original *Walbridge 1½* plate. None of the Cirencester, Stroud or Gloucester Folk museum items are on display but all are available on prior application for study and enjoyment.

On the eastern section, where much of the canal line remains on private property, two re-sited stones with plates intact *Walbridge 22* and *Walbridge 22 ½* can be viewed with permission at the entrance to Eisey Farm, half a mile down the farm access road and just beyond where the canal crossed. The worked and shaped area of the stone measures 32" in height above the rougher (and buried) base, with a width across the face of 13" and a side profile of 11½" at the base reducing to 10" where the round-head profile begins. The plate measures 11" in width and 13" in depth.

The milestone just above Bowbridge Lock (Walbridge 1) *is seen here being used to secure the dredging boat at work in the pound. This manual spoon dredging continued until the final days of the canal, and was captured here c.1911 by E. Temple Thurston when researching his book* The Flower of Gloster. *(Photo Michael Ware Collection courtesy Mrs E. Temple Thurston)*

industrial buildings which – formerly Bensons International Systems Ltd although empty at the time of survey – still occupy the large expanse of the Brimscombe Port site. Access into the Port is by following the road uphill past The Ship, alongside and round the splendidly re-furbished and landscaped Port Mill, and thence left at the fingerpost 'Port Foundry', down to cross over the Frome into the infilled Port area. Now a mixture of carparking and empty industrial buildings, Brimscombe Port demands a strong imagination to appreciate what a hive of activity this area must once have been.

Key Access Points

Stroud – Explorer 168 848051
Use town centre car parks; Cheapside is close to both canal and railway station, and both are close to Wallbridge. Bell Hotel alongside.

Road access (but usually with parking difficulties) is available at various points between Stroud and Chalford, by turning off the A419 road, including Bowbridge. Turn at British Oak Inn.

Brimscombe – Explorer 168 868023
Access from A419. Bus service to and from Stroud and Chalford. The Ship Inn makes an excellent stopping place for refreshments along this stretch.

6 Brimscombe Port into the Golden Valley

Brimscombe Port

The Port was the focal point of the life of the Thames & Severn. It was the headquarters and early meeting place of the proprietors of the Canal Company with a staff of upwards of seventeen clerks, apprentices, wharfmen, labourers and craftsmen. This activity can be appreciated from a glance at the 1826 scene at Brimscombe. The significance of the Port was, of course, its function as an inland port, the transhipment point between vessels of different gauges, principally the Severn trows and the western type of Thames barges. Locks up to this point from Stroud were built to one gauge, accommodating the vessels of the Severn; thereafter all the way to the Thames to a different gauge, accommodating the vessels of the upper reaches of the Thames.

This was not bad planning or hurried decision-making; in his original survey Robert Whitworth foresaw this as a solution to one of the more obvious problems of linking the two great rivers, each with its long-standing boat building traditions. Uniformity across the network did not exist, nor did anybody expect that to be provided. Traders using the canal system were familiar with transhipment ports (other good examples include Ellesmere Port and Stourport), and knew that a range of activities was to be undertaken at Brimscombe: the off-loading of goods from one vessel to another, storage of goods awaiting shipment, payment of dues, checking of gauges and cargoes so that the correct charges could be levied, and all other commercial matters required by the canal company, whose staff were accommodated there for the purpose. So the Port can be pictured as a hive of activity when functioning at its busiest. Urgency in transportation was not the defining factor as it might be regarded today.

In general terms, the locks on the Stroudwater and up to Brimscombe measure 68-69ft long by 16ft 1-2in wide. Thereafter they measure 90-93ft in length by 12ft 9in or 13ft in width. As a water economy measure introduced in 1841-1842 many of this latter group were reduced to 70ft by a shortening of the lock chamber and re-siting of the top gates. This was achievable because of the predominance of the narrow boats for much of the through traffic; their 70ft length required less water than the barges. Such boats were locally known as long boats rather than narrow boats, the latter essentially a term of the midland canals system. The lock at Bourne, the first above the Port, was a hybrid at 90ft in length by 16ft in width, in order to accommodate access to and from the canal company's Bourne boatyard for trows and vessels of the Severn. The study of traditional boats, such as the trow, around the coasts and along the river systems is a quite separate, detailed and indeed fascinating study, but there is no doubt that the promoters of the Thames & Severn were concerned to ensure that the maximum amount of traffic could be attracted onto their route and vessels accommodated accordingly. Several very useful studies are recommended amongst the Further Reading.

Brimscombe Port

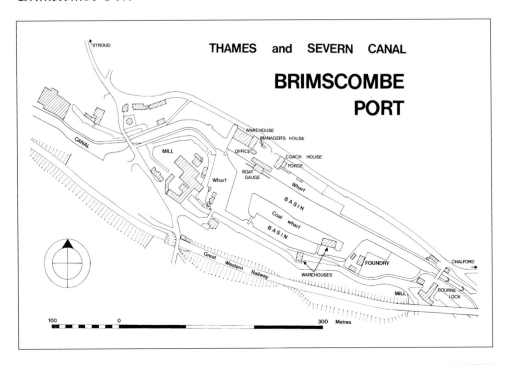

Brimscombe Port in 1826 from an illustration published in Delineations of Gloucestershire *with plates engraved by J. & H.S. Storer and text by J.N. Brewer. This fine view shows activity in the port, cranes and other facilities awaiting business and the warehouse building on the left.* (Photo courtesy Humphrey Household)

Brimscombe Port warehouse with the headquarters building on the right. (Photo courtesy Howard Beard Collection)

Brimscombe Port warehouse, after its conversion to Brimscombe Polytechnic in 1911. (Photo courtesy Stan Gardiner Collection)

The Port consisted of a large basin, about 700ft long and 250ft wide which a nineteenth-century commentator estimated could hold a hundred vessels. Plans show the layout: a central island storage area for coal and other goods susceptible to theft, and on the northern side the principal wharf with its main building. This was a remarkable structure containing warehouse, office and agent's house in three storeys; the records show that this was built by Thomas Cook from Painswick who was by trade a master mason, but who became a building contractor of some stature in the area. He had various contracts on the canal during its building period and also – incidentally – was responsible for the rebuilding works at Gloucester Jail during the same decade. Cook built the Port warehouse between 1786-1789 and the proprietors first met there the following year.

Also on this side of the wharf was a transit shed, a forge and later a boat-weighing machine. Given the importance of Brimscombe in the history of the Cotswold canals, it is a great pity that none of this now survives as the whole site was cleared some forty years ago for industrial use. Until recently the Port continued to function with a factory, a foundry and other activities; on the Port area proper all this has now ceased, although the refurbishment of Port Mill on the western side has brought new commercial enterprises into and around this fine building. The purchase of the Port area by British Waterways (with others) as these words were being written (July 2002) is a sign of a new generation of activity in prospect for Brimscombe Port. So, with hindsight, it is satisfying to note that it is just twenty years since the writers of the *Towpath Guide* deplored in particular the loss of the Port warehouse 'which would almost certainly have been the ideal base from which to launch the revival of interest in the canals across the Cotswolds'. Indeed, in a way, perhaps it has and it will.

The Brimscombe Port weighing machine is on the left, looking east up to Bourne Mill and bridge. This is one of the few views showing the full length and width of this part of the Port, c.1910. (Photo courtesy Howard Beard Collection)

Dismantling the weighing machine in June 1937. It was erected in 1845 to check frauds known to be practised by boatmen, avoiding the payment of tolls on the amount of goods carried in their vessels. It consisted of a cast-iron cradle in a massive superstructure. The boat was floated onto the cradle and the weight of boat plus cargo was recorded accurately when the water was run off by gravity. As a deterrent to toll evasion, it proved very successful and justified its cost of over £1,000. The design was based upon another example at Midford on the Somersetshire Coal Canal and a model produced for the committee's deliberations is preserved in Gloucester Folk Museum. (Photo courtesy Gloucestershire Record Office ref. PH1/1, copyright Stroud News & Journal)

In 1966 the Gloucestershire Society for Industrial Archaeology sponsored a plaque recording the significance of Brimscombe Port, and this was displayed on the works of Bensons International Systems Ltd with alongside it a replica mileplate *Walbridge 2½ Inglesham 26¼*. Following the takeover of the canal by Gloucestershire County Council in 1900, the warehouse was partly converted into a Polytechnic School in 1905 and then fully converted and officially opened in 1911. It became the Brimscombe Secondary Modern School under the Education Act of 1944 before finally moving to Eastcombe Manor School in 1962, following which these buildings were finally demolished in 1964.

Of the other remaining buildings in the Port, the two small cottages on the former western wharf, still occupied by a family directly linked to the old canal days, remained until the mid-1980s when they too were demolished. All that survives now is the adjoining (but separate) building, a salt store (note the ventilation slits in the upper walls), a token gesture maybe but one well worth having. The impressive buildings of Port Mill stand behind, a good example of the later nineteenth century rebuilding of stone mills in these valleys. It was a woollen mill until *c*.1920.

Brimscombe Port to Chalford

The route through the Port follows alongside the River Frome on the southern side and after a few minutes walk reaches Bourne Lock and Bridge. This was a hybrid lock built to the 90ft x 16ft dimension. Close to the lock stands Bourne Mill, and here is the classic spot to appreciate the close proximity of road, canal and railway, all competing for space along the valley; indeed the railway appears to cut right through the group of mill buildings. Still the home of a number of small businesses, the mill is still also known as Hack Mill; until a few years ago a painted sign on the upper floor read 'H.S. Hack Ltd., Stick Manufacturers, Bourne Mill'. The buildings here are further excellent examples of the great phase of mill rebuilding in the period 1825-1850 when the woollen cloth industry was at its height.

With the railway in close proximity, it is not surprising that a couple of the characteristic GWR boundary markers in cast iron can be found along this section. Above Bourne Lock the railway swings back across both valley and canal on a small low brick-arched viaduct, but the iron girder span over the canal has been underfilled and water is now channelled through pipes and the towpath diverted through an Armco tube. Across the canal the scant remains of the Thames & Severn Canal Company boatyard at the Bourne survived until recent years; now factory buildings cover the site. This yard was set up soon after the canal was opened, and was the scene of much boat-building and repairing activity; here vessels for both the Thames and the Severn traditions were constructed, plus the upkeep of the fleet of over fifty vessels which the company maintained during the period when it also acted as a carrying company. Conditions were fairly simple; boats were constructed in the dry dock (the earlier was roofed, the later was not) or on the bank of the canal, from where they were launched sideways into the cut.

Boats are moored up at the entrance to the boatyard at The Bourne, one of the focal points along the Thames & Severn for much of its life. (Photo courtesy Howard Beard Collection)

Delightful view of canal and railway side by side at Brimscombe station, with Beale's Lock and bridge in the foreground, looking west. The date is 1957, the station still functions in typical ex-GWR fashion and the canal is full of water above the lock (held back by a concrete barrier) to service the needs of the banker engines based at the station for Sapperton Bank duties. Although the canal is still there and in water today, all evidence of the station has vanished completely. (Photo Frank Lloyd, courtesy & copyright British Waterways Archives, Gloucester, ref. 5272)

On the towpath side stood Dark Mills, another mill complex with a variety of functions now gone – it was demolished in 1964. By the the now levelled bridge site stood Brimscombe Gas Works to which coal was brought directly by canal barge. It is now largely unrecognisable. Just beyond is a good example of a fine round-headed milestone (*Walbridge 3*).

Beale's Bridge and Lock provide more interesting details about the life of the canal. Firstly the bridge sits on the tail of the lock, almost but not quite a single unit, and a feature frequently found on the canal network. The bridge is smaller and seems more compact than others lower down, perhaps an indication of shortage of space here. So too the fact that the towpath does not pass under this bridge, so creating an inconvenience to the passage of boats, and requiring the unhitching of the towrope. Above the lock is the railway, just here about as close together as anywhere else along the valley. But it is a very different scene from the days when Brimscombe station was just through the gate, when this route over the bridge was regularly used for access across the railway to and from work along the towpath. Absolutely nothing appears to remain of the station, and still less (other than memories) of the stationing of banker engines in the small locomotive shed here to assist trains up the long bank to Sapperton Tunnel. The King & Castle provides one fixed point; it was previously the Railway Hotel. Road improvements have changed the landscape here too.

Ile's or Grist Mill Lock looking east up to Ballinger's Lock and the approach to Chalford wharf. The slatting on the lock gates is a Thames & Severn characteristic; the date 1908 on the lower gates is evidence of repair and refitting, and this view dates from not long afterwards. (Photo courtesy Howard Beard Collection, from an original postcard by F. Major of Bisley)

The strong dam built across the lock holds back a good depth of water in the next half-mile section up to St Mary's Lock. In the days of steam engines on the railway, the water level in this section of canal was used to supply water to the banker engines; even after abandonment of the canal in 1933 this arrangement still applied and is now one of the reasons why this stretch of canal and the dam remain in such good repair. This length represents one of the most attractive sections of canal along the valley, not least because it includes the approach to St Mary's Mill, a fine group of buildings as historic as any so far seen. The mill house stands behind. Both the 15ft hybrid waterwheel and a Tangye Compound steam engine installed second-hand in 1904 survive intact. Until 1986 walking sticks were still being made at this mill; following a disastrous fire in February 1979 the Chalford Stick Co. moved to a mill in Woodchester and the later Phoenix Walking Stick Co. also moved to Nailsworth. St Mary's Mill House has various associations of note including, it is believed, with Roger Bacon, the thirteenth-century discoverer of gunpowder. The access to the mill is interesting too, achieved via a tight descent from the main road across the only surviving manned railway crossing in the valleys, and certainly the most picturesque. The tiny crossing-keeper's cabin stands by the line; together with the GWR-style gates, it is a listed building now and survivor of more than one attempt to modernise it out of existence. It stands almost on top of the lock by the bridge.

Just before St Mary's Lock is one of the few places where there is direct level connection between the canal and river by means of a culvert under the towpath, another reason for the reasonable water levels in the canal along this length. The lock chamber is in good condition

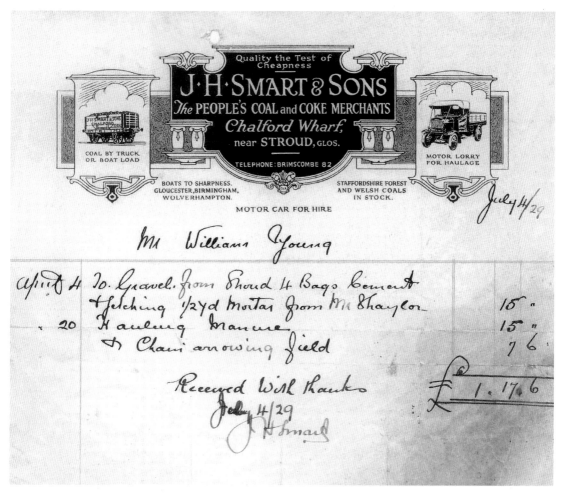

J.H. Smart & Sons were amongst the final carriers on the Stroudwater and Thames & Severn before closure of the latter beyond Stroud in 1933. Operating from Chalford Wharf, they supplied coal, coke and other goods along the canal line, before finally reverting to road haulage. This bill-head of July 1929 captures the period of transition – boat supplies are still advertised and the address remains Chalford wharf, wharf being originally a river and canal term but also later adopted by railway companies for their own yards. (Photo courtesy Museum in the Park Stroud, ref. CM.3594, copyright Stroud District (Cowle) Museum Trustees)

Although out of focus, this photograph taken in 1923 is a valuable record of a working boat alongside Smart's Chalford Wharf. Chalford Chapel Lock is in the left background and beyond the canal are the many mill buildings crowding this part of the Frome valley. (Photo Frank Lloyd, courtesy & copyright British Waterways Archives, Gloucester, ref. 5251)

but once again the railway comes back across the canal, the original bridge has been underfilled and the canal is culverted into a pipe creating another obstacle to restoration. The towpath is also diverted into a separate tube. From this point the locks come closer together as the canal climbs up the valley and, once through the footway, it is only a short distance to Ile's or Grist Mill Lock which still has remnants of its gates remaining in position. On the left-hand side, just before the lock, is Clayfield's Mill, now converted into housing; part of this site was cleared for road-widening in the mid-1960s. A small stream which emerges on the valley side powered a waterwheel in the mill and then entered the canal. Looking at the parapets of the bridges leading up to the road along this section, the additions in stone and brick become obvious where the tracks were sloped up to the new turnpike road built in 1814. Previously, these bridges were merely humpbacked over the canal. The site of Ile's Mill was below the towpath between canal and railway line; it was gutted by fire in 1913 and now all that remains is the house and a few odd buildings. Its other name derives from the Grist family who made flock and shoddy here over a century ago.

Chalford Wharf

Within one hundred yards, and emerging to cross over the road, is the site of Ballinger's Lock. The infilled chamber is now covered by a small row of three garages with the canal culverted into a pipe beneath. Road widening has taken its toll of the canal line, although the towpath is picked up again quickly and approaching Chalford wharf it formed the focus for a 'Stroud

Valley Facelift' project in the mid-1960s. The stone edging forming the wharf can be seen, and some still have iron mooring rings fixed to them. Chalford wharf was a busy place with many mills, both large and small, in fairly close proximity, and the canal widened out at this point to form a 'winding hole' or turning place for barges. Here is a reminder of one of the major problems which the Canal Company faced throughout its life; much of its trade was concentrated in the western section, and only a relatively small amount actually traversed the entire length of the Thames & Severn. Lucrative as this local western trade might be – particularly in coal carrying – the heavy maintenance costs of the long climb to the summit, the summit itself and the whole of the eastern section were set against the relatively meagre returns. When the other imbalance – a far greater movement eastwards of traffic than ever flowed westwards – is added, this gives some idea of the basic miscalculation of traffic flow which affected the financial well-being of the canal through much of its life.

The centrepiece of the wharf is undoubtedly Chalford roundhouse, the first of five such buildings to be seen on the Thames & Severn and a well-known feature of it *(private property)*. There is a special story to be told of the architectural interest of key buildings along this canal. These are examined separately in this study (see pp.112-114). Today the wharf represents a small but valuable amenity area; the pillars at the entrance from the road remain in situ, and nearby is the overflow weir which still carries surplus water into the River Frome. Prominently displayed is some of the sluice gear from Sevill's Mill further up the valley. Across the road stands

The little-photographed Chalford Chapel Lock is seen here at Easter 1933, within a few months of the canal's final closure in June. The lady is sitting on the lower gate beam looking back to the bridge, built at a skew to the canal, and constructed in red brick except for a section on the right which is built in stone to raise the parapet up to road level. All this was demolished and landscaped as part of road improvements in 1966 and the canal culverted through this section. (Photo Frank Lloyd, courtesy & copyright British Waterways Archives, Gloucester, ref. 5271)

the former Company's Arms Inn, which as Chalford Place dates back in part to the fifteenth century (it has an upper hall of that date), the very fine and typically Cotswold gables being added to the north side of the building by the seventeenth century. Derelict for some years, it is another example of a fine building now restored with some care *(private property)*. The Company's Arms forms the theme of a display in the new Museum in the Park in Stroud.

Beyond the roundhouse, a group of buildings face the wharf at right angles to the canal. The nearest one belonged to James Smart, barge master and coal merchant. His firm had its own fleet of barges trading on the canals and faded lettering on the north wall of the house still advertises this fact (what about restoring this, I wonder?). It remained for years a coal yard, although road transport had long since brought coal up from the railway at Stroud and elsewhere. It is up to this point that the western section of the canal remained at its most active even in a small way with Smart's barges trading right up to abandonment in 1933.

A rare view of the stone-built Bell Bridge at the bottom of Cowcombe Hill, where the main road to Cirencester crosses the canal line. Photographed in 1955, but later demolished for road improvements. (Photo Frank Lloyd, courtesy & copyright British Waterways Archives, Gloucester, ref. 5288)

Across the road is Chalford Church which as a chapel of ease gave its name to the next lock, Chapel Lock, where there was another small yard known as Whiting's Coal Yard just above the lock. This area was infilled in 1964 for road widening and improvements; the canal is culverted here, and one of the victims was the next milestone. However, built back into the culvert arch on the Chalford wharf side is the plate *Walbridge 4 Inglesham 24 ¾*. The towpath line follows behind the bus shelter through a good tree-lined walk. Road widening has taken about half of the canal bed. Behind the long stone wall to the towpath was the substantial group of buildings known as Bliss' Mill; once there were in fact five separate mill concerns here employing at their peak in excess of 1,000 people in the manufacture of walking sticks and other products, the majority of which were exported world-wide. The site now forms the Chalford trading estate and some of the older buildings survive amongst modern additions. The canal now winds past the last group of buildings of this more industrialised part of the route passing the modern canal-side works of Chalford Chairs, a woodworking mill for many years, and approaches the crossing of the main A419 Stroud-Cirencester road at the foot of Cowcombe Hill. Here the substantial Bell Bridge was built in stone in 1814 to carry the new turnpike road over the canal. Although it looks as though it too has fallen victim to road improvements, the bridge survives, but hidden; the River Frome is culverted deep under the canal here.

Key Access Points

Brimscombe – see Chapter 5

Chalford Wharf – Explorer 168 891025
There is some parking at the wharf which is set down from the A419, and limited parking in Chalford village; bus service to Stroud; shops and café.

7 Climbing to Daneway

The journey along the towpath from Stroud has never been far from the sight and sounds of the road. From the foot of Cowcombe Hill, the towpath suddenly takes off into another world, where the road noise seems to disappear and a tranquil walk of three miles along a good towpath is on offer all the way to the summit at Daneway. For many people, this section is by far the most rewarding of the entire experience of walking the old line of the Thames & Severn. Canal and River Frome continue as close companions, never far apart; sometimes the towpath forms an embankment between them, sometimes the river seems to disappear amongst the cottages and houses. Throughout it is apparent that the canal line was engineered through the valley at no great distance above the river – this is not a section for heavy cutting and embankment.

The built heritage of the valleys remains a feature, even as the sense of remoteness increases. Immediately on the roadside, at the point where Bell Bridge used to stand, is the nineteenth century Halliday's Mill, a brick and stone building still in use for various businesses but principally associated with the later years of the Arts & Crafts movement in Gloucestershire. In 1919 it was taken over by Peter de Waals, foreman to the Barnsley Brothers, furniture makers at Daneway House. Following the break-up of the group of craftsmen at Daneway, de Waals brought the workforce to this mill and carried on their traditional type of furniture-making until his death in 1937.

Bell Lock and Red Lion Lock

The towpath has now crossed from right to left. Some of the chamber of Bell Lock remains; this was one of the most photographed locks along this stretch of canal in Edwardian times. Just a little way up the hill stood Chalford railway station and goods yards, built in 1897, but this has all been swept away with almost no trace remaining of this busy little place. Bell Lock and Red Lion Lock are close together and take their names from nearby public houses, both reached by small footbridges across the River Frome on the left-hand-side. The Bell has disappeared completely although the New Red Lion remains in place of its predecessor and makes a good place to stop for refreshments.

At 4½ miles from Wallbridge, Red Lion Lock is significant in the history of the Thames & Severn in several ways. The original cutting of the line of the canal was advanced from west to east and had reached this point by the autumn or early winter of 1784, about eighteen months after the commencement of works. It enabled access to be gained to the 'Black Gutter', the local name for a group of springs in the valley side which were harnessed for canal use; hence we can assume that these and other sources were already 'in commission' when the first vessel is reported to have entered the locks at Wallbridge in January 1785. The significance is supported by the construction of a fine example of a stone bridge across the tail of the lock with its keystone inscribed 'CLOWS ENGr 1785'. Josiah Clowes was the

Bell Lock c.1910. The lock gates had been replaced in 1904; the date is marked on the beam. Two inns are seen in the photograph, Bell Inn on the left and Red Lion in the background; the latter survives.

Canal Company's 'surveyor, engineer and head carpenter' from 1783 and effectively the resident engineer putting Whitworth's proposals into effect on the ground. As he was very much in charge of the construction programme, it is not surprising to find this permanent record at Red Lion Lock. In fact, there is another, as the mason Herbert Stansfield had his own name and the date 4 December 1784 carved on the lock chamber – how interesting it would be if each lock bore such a useful record! The hillside tracks to which the Clows Bridge gave access were closed by the later railway construction close by; but certainly this stone bridge has a character all of its own which will not be seen elsewhere on the canal, although the bridge at Inglesham and the later stone bridge at Tarlton Road on the summit level also deserve special mention.

The milestone alongside the lock (*Walbridge 4½*) is a good example, and its plate has been preserved (see Milestones on p.68-69). The towpath is good in this section and well used. The steepness of the Chalford valley is very apparent here, with houses seeming to hang on the northern hillsides; just above to the south, the railway line is still climbing up the valley at a higher level than the canal with its own steep gradient all the way up Sapperton Bank, a mecca for railway photographers for generations. Both canal and railway curve round the now demolished woollen and silk mill known as Innell's or Sevill's Mill. These deviations were necessary to avoid the mill pond within the narrow confines of the valley, and discussions with the mill owners caused a six-month delay in the construction programme in 1785. The mill site is now a small community of houses, both modernised and new – the evidence of industry has all but disappeared, although the stone edge to the towpath remains where barges once tied up to bring coal and supplies to the mill.

Valley Lock is in the centre of this postcard view c.1910; Valley Inn is prominent to the left. (Photo courtesy Stan Gardiner Collection)

Valley Lock

Around the bend it is just a short distance to Valley Lock, or Golden Valley Lock, which together with the previous two locks has raised the canal through 26ft in just half a mile. Here is another little valley-side community, with cottages and houses close together. The finest is right by the lock and shares its name; formerly the Valley Inn, this fine late seventeenth century Cotswold stone house was originally a mill house and its first name as a pub was the Clothiers Arms. Now a *private residence,* lettering on the wall facing the canal still showed faintly until recent years. Restoration of this lock continues; the wooden bridge at its tail has long since been replaced by a more functional concrete structure. Just below, at the entrance to the playing fields, some stonework of the sluices from a sawmill can still be found. At this point the canal leaves the village of Chalford and the next section has a character all of its own for the 2¾ miles to Daneway and it is possible to imagine that the scene appears almost unchanged in the two centuries since the canal was built.

Above Valley Lock the towpath is shaded by a line of overhanging trees, which contribute to the peaceful woodland atmosphere along the canal bank. The large brick building on the opposite side dates from *c.*1890 and was the original Chalford Water Works, a typical industrial building with round-headed iron-framed windows. Coal supplies were delivered by canal for the steam-driven pumps. The building is still used as a small industrial concern. Along this section is another surviving canal milestone, also without its original plate (*Walbridge 5*) although a replica was installed in August 2002. The house in the fields below the canal is all that remains of Ashmead's Mill which once processed silk but was demolished in 1903. The incidence of silk mills in the valley shows that silk cloth production tended to take over from woollen cloth production when the latter was gradually lost to the larger Yorkshire mills which were prepared to modernise in order to remain competitive in the face of stiff competition. There may have been some complacency amongst the Stroud valley woollen mills and their owners.

Baker's Mill

A straight stretch follows, flanked by Westley and Oldhill Woods, for about half a mile up to Baker's Mill Lower Lock, which was also known as Bolting's Lock. A dam across the top of the lock backs water up to the next lock and it was the short-lived Thames & Severn Canal Trust which was responsible in 1897 for lining this pound with concrete to stop water leakage. It became known locally as the 'conk' and was used as a huge swimming pool. Another round-headed milestone (*Walbridge 5½*) can be found just before the stone-built Baker's Mill Upper Lock where the lane following along the valley from Chalford to Frampton Mansell crosses over the canal by a bridge now reinforced and without its earlier character; it sits right on the tail of the lock. Access from the road and very limited parking are available here, and a wooden footbridge crosses the lock. Close by was a small wharf at which coal was unloaded for Oakridge silk mill.

Below the lock is the mill house and surviving buildings of Baker's or Twissell's Mill, the latter named after a seventeenth century clothing family. It later became a corn mill. Immediately above the mill and covering the mill pond the Thames & Severn Canal Co. bought land and constructed a large reservoir as a source of water to the locks lower down. This had become necessary because of the failure of the arrangements at Sapperton and particularly of a smaller reservoir at Daneway. This location gave access to springs, feeding into the leated river, and this was virtually the only place of sufficient size high enough up the valley to be of use as a reservoir, and therefore the company was almost forced to buy this land and then to acquire Puck Mill just further up the canal (putting it out of business) in order to guarantee the water supply to fill the reservoir. At almost 900ft in length, 94ft in

Looking west from the bridge at Baker's Mill c.1890 before this section was concreted a few years later. The quarry in the background, now tree-covered, is at the bottom of Drivers Wood. (Photo courtesy R.L.M. Allen, Prestwich)

width and 6ft in depth, it has a capacity of more than 3 ¼ million gallons. Like the mill, the present lake is *private*, supports plenty of wildlife, has private fishing and is a most attractive feature. This whole area is very rural and peaceful, with the wooded slopes of the valley coming down to the water's edge.

The towpath runs between reservoir and canal as a raised path and in wet winter weather there can be a great deal of water on both sides. This section remains scenically one of the most interesting along the canal at any season of the year. Once the canal clears the end of the reservoir the two locks at Puck Mill appear quite close together; higher up, the railway viaduct crosses a small side valley with the village of Frampton Mansell on the skyline. The canal is usually quite dry here above the level of the reservoir and the pound between the Puck Mill Lower and Upper Locks was a constant worry to the Canal Company as it leaked very badly, losing water almost as quickly as it received it. This pound was therefore the scene of a considerable reconstruction effort in 1907 by Gloucestershire County Council, which had taken over the canal in 1900. Over a three-month period, the canal bed was completely stripped out and re-puddled with clay in the traditional manner. A series of photographs survives of these activities and, apart from minor details, the scenes appear little different from those a visitor to the original construction might have witnessed 120 years previously. In both cases, virtually the entire operation was undertaken by hand. This was the last of the large-scale work sites on the canal before it fell into disuse in the second decade of last century. No boats passed this way after 1911, with complete abandonment following in 1933. The top end of the Lower Lock was blocked off for use as a swimming pool some years ago.

The intensive programme of reconstruction work at Puck Mill Lower Lock in 1907, with Baker's Mill in the background. The processes of relining the pound and repairing the lock can clearly be seen. (Photo courtesy Humphrey Household)

Puck Mill

At Puck Mill Upper Lock the towpath changes to the right-hand-side via a bridge at the tail of the lock. This must have been an interesting little community gathered in the valley floor, with the canal as a focus. The canal's construction obviously split up the limited farming land in the valley, hence the need for an 'accommodation' bridge to link up the several portions. Its siting immediately below the lock allowed both access on the level and gave the canal boats below sufficient headroom to pass before entering the lock, which rises here 8ft. The lock gates were amongst the group replaced in 1902/1903, and old photographs taken along the line of the canal in this period often show these dates incised on the new gates.

The four-storey Puck Mill itself has long gone; it fell into disuse before 1865. A mill on this site is recorded from 1572, a grain mill later converted to a cloth mill. It was owned by Samuel Bidmead when the Thames & Severn Company bought it in 1791 in order to improve its water control. The company sold it in 1804 but the influence of such an imposing building in this narrow valley survives even now. In recent years all of the remaining buildings at Puck mill have been modernised. Road access to this area remains via a track under the railway viaduct from the nearby road, replacing an even more adventurous approach directly down from Frampton Mansell village. Walking through this area, please remain on the towpath and respect *private property*. The barn with its blocked-up windows identified in the 1984 *Towpath Guide* is now a private house, with extensions, and now looks very different from its earlier purpose as the Oak Inn, the only pub up the line between Chalford and Daneway, whose customers were almost totally derived from the canal. Above the mill site is

Licensee Samuel Elliott with his wife Emily stand at the gate of The Oak Inn at Puck Mill; this view was taken from the bridge across Puck Mill Upper Lock. The inn sign advertises Beer, Ales and Porter. (Original photograph by Henry Lockyer, courtesy John Stanley from collection of Mrs Pat Sullivan)

With only minor changes of detail, these views of work in progress on Puck Mill Lower Lock in 1907 replicate the way in which the canal must have been built and repaired throughout its life. A gang of workmen and their foreman stand in the top of the lock chamber. The gates seal against the stout wooden arrow-shaped elm baulks forming the sill of the lock. The second group is puddling clay to renew the canal bed. The canal was closed for three months from 19 August in that year for this work to proceed. (Photos courtesy Humphrey Household, one from an original photograph by Henry Lockyer)

This postcard captures the charm and isolation of Puck Mill c.1903, showing the decayed state of the Upper Lock, with gates in poor state. The sign of the Oak Inn can just be seen on the left. The caption suggests an overprinting and re-issuing of this earlier photograph, once repair work had begun. (Photo courtesy Stan Gardiner Collection from an original by W. Dennis Moss of Cirencester)

The isolated cottage at Puck Mill, alongside Whitehall Lower Lock in 1938. The canal is completely dry. (Photo Frank Lloyd, courtesy & copyright British Waterways Archives, Gloucester, ref. 4195)

the former mill house and beyond the retaining walls of Puck Mill wharf the canal briefly opens out again as it approaches Whitehall Lower Lock and another cottage, once Puck Mill Farm, also brought back to life in recent years. A Thames & Severn Canal property boundary stone has been rebuilt into the quoins of this property (*not accessible*).

Whitehall to Daneway

The canal now swings round in an arc, leaving the stream and crossing the valley floor to the northern bank. Only with great difficulty can the former millpond for Puck Mill be recognised. From here to Daneway, a distance of almost a mile, there are no more houses in the valley. The towpath is an enjoyable and popular walk, although the canal bed is largely overgrown from the woods which tumble down the hillside on the far bank. The next feature of note is the brick and stone Whitehall Bridge, isolated in the valley floor. This remains an impressive structure, with much evidence of its repair and rebuilding (it is now almost an even mixture of both). Another accommodation bridge, it served the several rough tracks and footpaths which cross at this point. On the lower side a fine (if decaying) date stone reads *W.D. 1784* – presumably the contractor-mason William Dennis, who was also responsible for work on two of the next group of locks up the line. Even so, the date 1784 seems early in the sequence of building the canal – perhaps this was the section worked on whilst the delay at Innell's Mill held up proceedings further down? Whitehall Bridge was the point selected as demarcation for the official abandonment of the canal to the east in 1927; the section up to this point from Wallbridge was not officially abandoned until 1933.

It also marks the beginning of the Sapperton valley reserve of the Gloucestershire Wildlife Trust, leased from the Bathurst estate as owners. Just above the bridge is another milestone, this time flat-topped (*Walbridge 6½*) and soon Whitehall Upper Lock is reached along a straight section; this can be considered as the bottom of a flight of seven locks all within the next half-mile up to the summit level at Daneway. This was often (perhaps always?) a difficult section to work with a fully-laden boat, particularly as the records show the struggle to maintain a good level of water in the pounds between the locks. In fact, there is a good case that these pounds – really reservoirs – were built too short to contain the amount of water required to fill each lock. In the final 1½ miles up to the summit there are no less than eight locks. Evidence of significant attempts to reduce the quantity of water required can be seen. A series of major improvements were carried out along the line of the canal following recommendations made in 1820, although it was not until 1841 that most of the locks in this section were shortened by about 20ft with the insertion of a masonry arch across part of the lock chamber, the top gates being then re-hung. Consumption was thus reduced by up to 20%. The original length of these locks (90-93ft) was of course determined by the length of the Thames barges, but as most of the traffic was by then carried by the shorter 70ft narrow boats (or longboats) of the midland canals this improvement could be carried out without loss of trade.

Indeed, the need for water retention led also to the building of a series of side-ponds to the top five locks up to Daneway and these were probably all completed in 1823. At a depth of 3ft and capable of holding up to 2,500 cubic yards capacity each, these ponds helped considerably in the constant battle against water loss. Their remains can still be made out

In the flight of locks below Daneway at Siccaridge Wood and Bathurst Meadow. In this view by Henry Taunt of Oxford, perhaps c.1910, the canal bed is dry and there is no activity. (Photo courtesy Centre for Oxfordshire Studies, copyright Oxfordshire County Council)

amidst the undergrowth along this section – look particularly for the retaining bank on the offside at the approach to each lock. They remain on *private property* so should only be studied from the towpath.

Bathurst Meadow Lock is next and here the towpath again crosses over, from right to left; the present wooden bridge is the successor to others in this position. None of this group of locks retains its gates and all are overgrown; damage to the lock chambers from tree growth is obvious and restoration here may well require substantial rebuilding in due course. This is the steepest part of the valley and the locks are named after Sickeridge (or Siccaridge) Wood which seems to hang above the walker coming up the towpath. This wood and Daneway Banks further up are also Gloucestershire Wildlife Trust reserves. Hence in quick succession, Sickeridge Wood, Lower, Middle and Upper Locks, each rising 8ft 5in with no more than 300 yards between them.

The valley at last opens out a little and this allowed just enough space for the wharf and basin, which stands alongside Daneway Basin Lock. Access was just above the lock, where the canal opens out into an almost circular and stone-edged turning pound with the wharf entrance off to the right; here boats moved to load or unload their cargoes, mostly of coal, stone and timber. The basin was also used for barges to 'lay-up' whilst awaiting their turn to proceed and pass through the tunnel, navigation of which was controlled on an alternating four-hourly basis both night and day. The basin also served as a reservoir supplying water to the flight of locks down the valley, supported by the other measures already noted. At some later date the basin was lined with concrete and this lining still remains in reasonable order and has recently been exposed in the landscaping of the wharf area. Derelict into the 1980s,

The community at Daneway, where the canal reaches the summit. In the centre is the wharf cottage with the open expanse of wharf in front; the basin is to the right. The tall brick chimney of the sawmill is partially hidden by trees; on the skyline, Sapperton church spire can just be seen.

Daneway wharf with the Bricklayers Arms in the background. Annie Hyett (born in 1874) and on the left of the two ladies standing at the wharfside, was visiting relatives down the valley in Chalford from her home in Bath. (Photo courtesy Stan Gardiner Collection)

Unusual view of the top lock at Daneway, now buried to form the car park of the inn alongside. This view dates from c.1911 and comes from the album of Temple Thurston, inspiration for his journey in The Flower of Gloster. *(Photo Michael Ware Collection courtesy Mrs E. Temple Thurston)*

the small wharfinger's cottage has since been rescued, modernised and extended. The now renamed Wharf Cottage and the whole wharf area is *private property*, although most of the features of the wharf can be studied from the roadside at Daneway Bridge or by walking a little way up the lane to Bisley from the road junction.

Like Puck Mill, Daneway was another canal-side community with its own individual history. The canal had been cut as far as Daneway by the summer of 1786, nearly three years before the tunnel itself was completed. Thus this little hamlet became a hive of activity with the establishment of wharf, warehouse and coalyard, plus the construction of the road now running up the valley side to the village of Sapperton higher up. Hence goods could be carried by canal this far and transferred for road transport to Cirencester and beyond. Immediately beyond the bridge was Daneway Summit Lock, where the canal reached the summit level. The total rise has been 241ft from Wallbridge through twenty-eight locks. Again, the towpath changes sides, and the lock itself has been almost completely infilled to form a car park for the Daneway Inn alongside. This building too has canal significance for it was built by the canal contractor John Nock in 1784 as a base and accommodation for his men working on the construction of the tunnel just around the corner. It was sold out of the Canal Company's ownership in 1807 to become the Bricklayer's Arms inn and has been a public house ever since. It was renamed the Daneway Inn in 1947.

Nearby stood a sawmill, originally water powered, but later converting to steam. It was worked by the Gardiner family, one of its products being barrel staves for the Birmingham market. Local memory recalls these journeys by canal being completed by the return of

Staffordshire coal for sale locally. Of the mill there are no remains except a few stones from the sluice gear, although its chimney can often be seen in old photographs. The bridge and causeway across the valley at Daneway was the centre of local controversy in 1979 when the stability of the bank and bridge was found to need strengthening. The levelling down of both was only avoided by considerable local as well as Canals Trust opposition, which led to a reprieve and the listing of the Daneway bridge (perhaps now is the time to review such protection for all the Thames & Severn Canal's bridges?).

To approach the tunnel, follow the footpath sign 'Sapperton' from the bridge via a small stile into the field below the car park (*not* through the car park) and this soon leads back to the towpath. Across the field the line of the canal shows very well and construction methods can be appreciated; the canal is cut into the slope of the hill and the spoil thrown over to form an embankment along which the towpath runs. The bed is quite deep as the summit level was intended to hold 6ft of water and be built to a greater width than lower down, both factors contributing to its capacity as a reservoir. However, problems of leakage involved the company in a constant struggle to hold even 4ft of water along the summit level. The embanked towpath rounds some bends before the last point where the River Frome is culverted under the canal; this is right on the bend where the line turns away from the river valley and heads directly into the hillside and Sapperton Tunnel. This is a good place to appreciate that the tunnel was surveyed first, and the line of the canal then engineered to meet it.

Just before the tunnel entrance stood a lengthman's cottage, which has steadily deteriorated over thirty years to the ruin it now is; the *Towpath Guide* in 1984 recorded it as 'alas seriously vandalised; the building is unsafe and must have a doubtful future, although it would be a pity to lose this link with the history of the tunnel'. Indeed so. The rectangular cottage was lived in until the early 1970s despite the absence of any main services. Right against the tunnel entrance is the last milestone on the western section (*Walbridge 7½*). From alongside, a track leads up to the Daneway-Sapperton road and provides a point of access to this section. Another footpath over the top of the tunnel portal strikes obliquely up the hillside to Sapperton village, which is well worth a visit and is another point of access.

Key Access Points

Chalford – see Chapter 6
This is an excellent starting point for the towpath walk (free of roads) up to Daneway and back (round trip of six miles).

Intermediate access is difficult; limited parking at *Baker's Mill*.

Daneway – Explorer 168 939034
Excellently placed to provide a base for canal exploration, either up to the tunnel or perhaps most useful of all as one end of the Chalford-Daneway walk which is scenically probably the most interesting and accessible section of the entire canal. Roadside parking, plus parking in the Daneway Inn car park *for patrons only* – an excellent spot for refreshments, where the mood of the old canal days still lingers.

8 Sapperton Tunnel

Building the tunnel

Sapperton Tunnel is certainly the most impressive achievement in the construction of the Thames & Severn and it was also the most difficult and expensive. The story of its building in 1784-1789 is intimately tied up with both success and failure. At first the Canal Company made the error of contracting with one Charles Jones to undertake the work; although well recommended, Jones proved to be over-ambitious and incapable of such a major task with responsibility for driving a tunnel over two miles long with twenty-five vertical shafts. He was described as 'neither a skilful artist, attentive to his business or honourable, but vain, shifty and artful in all his dealings'. His dismissal was protracted and accompanied by bitter wrangles. The proprietors realized their error in appointing one individual and replaced him with five groups of new contractors who continued the tunnelling. The records show that among these were John Nock and Ralph Shepperd, who had constructed so much else of the line, and they finished the job. This is one reason why it all took so long, but it is quite easy today to under-estimate the scale of the achievement. In the later eighteenth century, tunnelling on this scale was still a rarity and Sapperton has still only been overtaken in length of tunnelling by two other canal tunnels and ten tunnels of the later railway age. The agreed length for Sapperton is 3,808 yards (although others have 3,817 yards). Standedge across the Pennines is 5,698 yards (recently re-opened) and Strood in Kent (now a railway tunnel) is 3,946 yards.

The actual depth below the surface is 200ft in places and the tunnel is large at 15ft diameter, a considerable factor in adding to its grandeur. Until the blockages occurred, it was possible from one position to see right through the tunnel. This was cut originally with a smaller tunnel to create the headway. Completed early in 1787, it was then enlarged to the full size. In surveying the original line, Robert Whitworth confessed that the tunnel would be 'an uncertain piece of business in point of expense' because of the nature of the rock, and his estimate of £36,575 was considerably exceeded.

A most useful contemporary account is reported in Simeon Moreau's *A Tour to Cheltenham Spa*, which ran through several editions. In the third edition in 1788 [pp.142-45] he includes an 'Account of the Great Tunnel' taken from 'some Gentlemen who went from Cheltenham October 7th 1786', a time when the works were at their most extensive.

> *From Cheltenhan to Park Corner (by the new road) 15 miles, [here bait] go one mile farther to Saperton, where is one of the entrances of the Great Tunnel, which forms part of the communication between the Severn and Thames rivers.*
>
> *From Stroud to Saperton, the canal is finished. The hill through which this subterraneous navigation is to pass, is about two miles and a quarter in length; at the Saperton end they have penetrated about 400 yards, at the other half a mile; but there are pits formed the whole length of the hill, at the distance of 220-30 or 40 yards, where are at this time eight gangs working, in order to make the communication the quicker, and it is supposed the whole of what is finished in two years and a half, since the work was begun, may be about a mile. The labourers work by the*

yard, and rent it of the grand contractor at the rate of £4 14s 6d to £5 10s a yard; out of which they find candles, gunpowder, and labour, both for arching and clearing the passage. The bricks are burnt on the spot, and the brick-work carried on as they go.

The dimensions of the arch in the clear, 13 feet by 15 high; and below the base of it is a concave pavement, about 18 inches in the centre, of bricks placed with the ends downwards, and ramm'd very hard into the earth. The brickwork about 12 or 18 inches thick.

A small tunnel four feet square is first carried on to drain off the water from the larger one, and makes the work easier. There is a small tunnel at the extremity of the large one, at the Saperton end.

The soil is a blue marle, very hard, and worked with gunpowder; here they penetrate about eight yards in a fortnight; in which time they consume £3 10s worth of gunpowder but as they have met with a great deal of rock in some of the pits, it will impede their progress, and make the work of the whole, on an average, not more than two yards an half a week for each gang, or twenty yards a week for the 8 gangs, which is the utmost.

The first contractor receives £7 a yard from the company, which makes the whole expences £30,800 for 4400 yards.

As they pass the pits they have a funnel in each to admit air. The number of men who can work at the same time are:

3 miners
2 fillers of waggons
2 drivers, and
1 person to empty the waggon.

There is a stage or platform laid for the wheels of the waggon to run on, and from a shoulder which is given to the wheel, the waggon (which is made on the construction of a truck) is prevented from slipping off. The wheels are one piece of solid wood.

They never blow away more than two loads at a time, so keep only one waggon employed. They seldom meet with springs, having only found one in the 400 yards on the Saperton side; but the damp is such that it must subject the people to agues; they say, however, they are as strong and hearty as they should be above ground. The distance from the top of the arch to the surface of the hill is from 70 to 90 yards.

The different gangs working in the tunnel have sometimes two and sometimes three reliefs, and they work eight hours at a time, day and night, Sunday not excepted.

The Stroud canal enters the Severn at Framilode, and is eight miles in extent. It communicates with the Isis canal, which is thirty miles in length, and empties itself into the Isis at Lechlade.

At the distance of a quarter of a mile below Saperton is Denway, where there are seven locks, well worth seeing. In your return from them leave Saperton on the left, and on the right you will see a line of thirteen pits or shafts equally divided from Saperton to Heywood, the other extremity of the subterraneous navigation.

By a letter received from Cirencester, April 15th, 1788, I find there still remain 700 yards of the large tunnel, and about 130 yards of the small tunnel to finish, which may be completed in a year; but will more likely take up near twice that time.

The whole length of the canal, including the collateral cut, is 30 miles, and of the tunnel, (according to this letter) 3880 yards.

Moreau was Master of the Ceremonies at Cheltenham from 1780 until his death in December 1801. His guide went through a number of editions between 1783 and 1805, providing a useful contemporary source for far more than the canal. For example, he mentions 'the new road' – at this time turnpike trusts were also seeking to improve the road network and so compete for local trade. There is also an interesting reference in this account to the early use of a railway at Sapperton when digging the tunnel.

Navigating the tunnel

It will immediately be obvious that there was no towpath through the tunnel. At the time Sapperton was built, such sophistications were yet to come, and – despite its width – the bore of the tunnel still allowed for only a single line of wide-beam traffic, hence the timetable for its use. Entry was restricted to fixed times, effectively on a four-hourly cycle day and night, so that no more than three passages in each direction were possible within a twenty-four-hour period. So delays were inevitable just waiting for the time to enter, and complaints grew to a point where the company decided to open the tunnel at night, even though they, like other canal companies, only opened the rest of the canal during the day. Over the long life of the tunnel access arrangements did vary. *Bradshaw's Canals and Navigable Rivers of England and Wales* in 1904, for example, quotes the access arrangements at that time as 'boats enter the west end of the tunnel at 12 noon and the east end of the tunnel at 7am and 6pm, except on Sundays'.

The method of working boats through has become part of canal legend. They were 'legged' by men lying on the roof or prow of the boat and walking against the tunnel side or springing off the roof arch. On the broader Thames barges, this was easier to achieve than on the narrower boats in common use in later years, when a plank was extended on which the legger lay. The use of sticks or poles – 'Shafts or Sticks or other Things' – against the tunnel walls to propel boats was forbidden, although it was no doubt employed surreptitiously as a technique and there are occasional references to 'tunnel sticks' for the purpose.

It is one of the great stories attached to the Thames & Severn Canal that 'leggers' were available (as they were on tunnels elsewhere) to undertake this back-breaking work, spending their time in readiness and preparation in the pubs at either end of the tunnel. How much of this is fact and how much fiction would require some detailed research, but certainly no log or anything similar survives to authenticate this procedure, which may well have happened as an essentially casual and ad-hoc business anyway. Whilst all this was in progress, the horses – or more usually a pair of donkeys – followed the footpaths over the summit from one tunnel entrance to the other. These paths are still known as 'the donkey path' and can still be followed for the greater part.

However it was done, how long did it take to pass through Sapperton Tunnel? In the eastbound direction (entering at Daneway), many journeys were made against the flow of water from Thames Head pumping station, which slowed progress to about five hours; in the westbound direction (entering at Coates) this time might be reduced to three hours. Some twentieth-century movements give variations, although each might be untypical. In 1904 Joseph Hewer took *Staunch* through in 3 ¼ hours 'by means of tunnel sticks' forbidden in the old days; Temple Thurston's (fictional?) journey in 1911 took him four hours legging, but a few years later Bonthron took *Balgonie* through in ninety-five minutes, pulling with boat hooks to a wire fixed to the wall – itself no doubt an (undated) improvement made some years before.

Today the tunnel is blocked, most particularly in two places where large falls of rock (believed to be in 1969) effectively severed the through route. The tunnel remains *private property and also remains in a dangerous condition.* Unauthorised access into it from either end is both dangerous and unwise – far better to take advantage of the Canals Trust seasonal trip-boat from the Coates end, which is a memorable experience. The geology of the Cotswold hills at this point goes a long way in explaining some of the problems of maintenance in the tunnel. From the western or Sapperton entrance, a section runs through the notoriously unstable fuller's earth which had to be lined with brick and stone; a further section cut through the inferior oolite and remained unlined and spectacularly rock-cut. In the next long section through fuller's earth, lining was again required and this became known as the Long Arching. Such lines of geological fault between these beds were themselves points of weakness. Restoration of the tunnel will form the major challenge in the overall restoration in due course and also be its crowning achievement. There have been several engineering feasibility studies commissioned on the potential for re-opening, and each has accepted that this could be done with modern methods and technology, but always at a substantial cost.

The Western or Daneway portal

The canal around the western entrance has been the subject of work-parties to tidy up the area, and undertake some masonry repairs, but the most significant achievement to date has been the restoration of the tunnel portal or façade, completed and unveiled in September 1996. The victim of a great deal of vandalism over the years, this façade has now been returned to its former impressive state, a battlemented entrance full of gloom and foreboding, presenting a sombre image to the canal traveller. The sense of awe with which for more than a century boatmen entered the tunnel into the darkness can still be appreciated.

This whole area has been well-photographed over the years, an attractive scene with the lengthman's cottage alongside the tunnel entrance, its access either along the towpath or down a track from the nearby road. Right by the tunnel entrance, where the towpath finally comes to an end, is the milestone for *Walbridge 7½*, another with its plate removed in recent years.

Amongst the surviving records from the period of canal construction is a specification for the work undertaken to build the Daneway portal, for the mason Edward Edge, who was paid by the cubic foot. It is worth repeating verbatim:

Measure of the stone work at the Sapperton end of the tunnel, March 1785

To Arch in end of Tunnel
To Stones at end of Arch rustick 16 times
To Key stone for first circle
To Wing part up to Springing of Arch
To – ditto – other side
To wings up to Crown of Arch – double ditto

Perhaps one of the best-known postcard views along the Thames & Severn Canal, at the Daneway entrance to Sapperton Tunnel, captured by Cirencester photographer W. Dennis Moss c.1902. The pair of stone cottages at the entrance to the tunnel were lived in until the 1970s despite being some way from the nearest road. The building's subsequent collapse removes another link with the canal at work.

To above Crown of Arch to top of Breaks at the face of the Tunnel
To coping on the backside of face of Tunnel
To backside of Battlements
To inside of Battlements
To Base under middle pinacle
   To Cap
   To ditto
To pinacle
To pinacles at one end, To Base double
   To Cap
   To ditto
   To pinacle
To Foundation of Bond Walls to top of Coping of Wing Walls – double
To coping wall at end of Tunnel
To ditto other wall
Total   3070ft 2in cu.ft

For 'dressing and setting' of which he was paid £64 9s 4d
Total payment (for materials plus above) £162 5s 4d

Sapperton to Coates (above the tunnel)

Two routes are on offer to begin the 2½ mile walk over the tunnel from the Sapperton portal to the Coates entrance. A track leads up to the right to join the road up from Daneway into Sapperton, but an alternative route crosses the top of the portal and climbs directly up to Sapperton village, its church spire on the horizon. The attractions of this archetypal village in Cotswold stone are immediately obvious. Well known as a focus for Arts & Crafts activity at the turn of the nineteenth-twentieth centuries, it remains a fine example of conservation in stone. The churchyard of St Kenelm contains the graves of Ernest Gimson and Ernest and Sidney Barnsley, well-known exponents of the William Morris tradition of simplicity in everything.

Either of the two routes leaving Sapperton towards Cirencester will reach the section of road where views to the south across the small valley to Hailey Wood beyond include sight of several large clumps of beech trees. These mark the line of the tunnel, and are in fact the spoil tips marking the position of vertical shafts dug down to the canal level and used as fixed points from which the horizontal cutting was carried out. In deference to the wishes (implied if not expressed) of the landowner Earl Bathurst, the canal proprietors arranged for these spoil heaps to be planted with beech trees and they now form a very distinct and attractive feature of the local landscape. This was and remains a sensitive landscape; the Broad Ride which is a principal feature of the grade-one listed Cirencester Park crosses just here. This straight tree-

Inside Sapperton Tunnel, showing stone and brick lining. (Photo courtesy Cotswold Canals Trust)

lined avenue extends some five miles through the Park from Sapperton Common all the way to Cirencester, and is itself a superb walk on another occasion.

No right of way exists along the actual line of the shafts and spoil tips. The view across the fields can be fixed on the modern bungalow of Tumbledown in the bottom, beyond which a scrub-covered mound in the field marks one of the shafts. The bungalow stands virtually on the line of the tunnel. Some of the spoil heaps here reveal the grey material of the fuller's earth beds below. Although all the shafts were originally filled, some were reopened at the end of the nineteenth century for repair work and *remain dangerous structures to be left well alone.* At least one remains an open tunnel shaft, perhaps left open for ventilation purposes and now lined by stone walling. There are numerous routes through Hailey Wood, but the easiest to follow is the Macmillan Way long-distance footpath route, which crosses the fields and enters the wood close to the tunnel line, passing close to several air shafts. Use of OS maps or Way trails is especially recommended for this delightful woodland walk. Once under the railway bridge the track soon emerges from the wood alongside the Tunnel House Inn to join the Monarch's Way. From the inn car park, access can be regained back down to the towpath.

The Eastern or Coates portal

The Coates portal of the tunnel also remains an impressive structure and probably it was always intended to be so, to act as something of a showpiece for the Thames & Severn. The detailing is classical in style; indeed it seems to represent a sort of check-list of classical features one might expect to see: a central pediment with flanking classical columns and finials, two niches, plus two circular roundels and a central rectangular entablature. All this sits atop the actual tunnel mouth which is set well down into the cut. As with the western portal, a specification of work survives for the Coates portal too, in this case in the name of Thomas Cook, mason.

Measure of the Stone Work at the Entrance of the Coates Field end of the Tunnel, November 1786

Arching the tunnel at the Coates Field End, further than R. Shepperd Arched, 35 cubic yards
Walls from the Entrance of the Tunnel down by the side of the Canal
Arch stones
Key stone
Plinths
Base
Columns
Capitals
Sills under the Niches
Niches
Circular tablets
Square ditto

Architrave & Frieze

Cornice

Plinths under the Beehives

Base under ditto

Beehives

Plinths under the Entablature

Front of the ditto

Sides of the ditto

Cornice of the ditto

Back of the ditto

Coping upon the Blockin Course

Wormholed stone in the front set in mortar

Blockin course ditto

South side wing

North side wing

Backing of the Front Wall

NB. Front Wall, 3 ½ thick set in mortar

Paid:

For 'dressing stone for the Tunnell, used in R. Shepperd's Work at the Coats field end'
£20 16s 6d

Getting and dressing stone for the use of Arching the Tunnel £331 19s 0d

Doing the stone work at Coates Field end of the Tunnel £86 8s 1d

The result was very striking and remains so, particularly since the Trust made the bold and enterprising decision to raise funds for the restoration of the portal in 1976-1978. The full story has been told elsewhere (see Further Reading) but at a cost of something over £6,000 local mason Bruce Russell with the aid of a job creation team undertook the recovery of

The eastern or Coates portal of Sapperton Tunnel on the Thames & Severn Canal Company's copper halfpenny token, designed and produced by Hancock of Birmingham in 1795. (Photo courtesy Humphrey Household).

Fully restored, the Coates portal in 1977. (Photo courtesy Abbey Studios Cirencester)

The inn at Tunnel House in the spring sunshine of 13 April 1947, very much in the external condition in which it was built. (Photo courtesy Humphrey Household)

much of the masonry from the canal bed, its repair and re-use. A relatively small amount of new stone was used, which has now blended in with the original. The formal unveiling by Earl Bathurst in July 1977 remains one of the highlights of restoration to date, and this whole section continues to do its job as an examplar of what can be achieved by amenity improvements as a precursor to full restoration. Seasonal trip boats offer the experience of a short journey into the tunnel, the beginning of greater things to come. Meanwhile, it has to be said that – twenty-five years on – the façade is once again showing signs of decay and deterioration.

Immediately above the portal, the Tunnel House inn, like the Daneway inn, also belongs to the construction period of the canal, both being built as accommodation for workers. It was then called the New Inn and had a range of stabling behind the inn, all now cleared away. Perhaps the greatest tragedy was a severe fire in 1952 which gutted the building. Reconstruction over several years produced the building as it now is without its original third floor, which served as lodging accommodation. Accessed only down a ¼-mile-long track (the condition of which has long been a local topic of conversation), the inn remains one of those off-the-beaten-track pubs so beloved of journalists and writers, in this case deservedly so as it still retains a special character isolated between woods and the open Cotswold countryside.

After the disastrous fire in January 1952, the shell of the building remained unrestored for a number of years, before completion in 1959 without its third storey. (Photo courtesy Corinium Museum Cirencester ref. 1981/131)

Key Access Points

Daneway – see Chapter 7

Tunnel House Inn at *Coates* – Explorer 168 966006.
Excellently placed to provide a base for canal exploration, along the King's Reach and sections of the summit level. Turn off the Coates to Tarlton road at the pub sign just before the bridge and follow the track. Inn car park *for patrons only* – an excellent spot for refreshments, where the solitude of the old canal days can still be appreciated.

Visitors to Sapperton Tunnel – 'a stupendous and curious work'

The construction of such an impressive structure as a canal tunnel over two miles long attracted much interest during the five years of its construction from 1784-1789, of which the visit of King George III on 19 July 1788 is perhaps best known. Some of the descriptions also give useful information about the progress being made and the equipment and materials being used.

1786
The *Gentleman's Magazine* [56, 1786, 926] carried a report of the work of a correspondent who provided sketches of each portal to the tunnel 'made about a month ago' [4 October 1786]. He was enthusiastic about these 'entrances to a stupendous and curious work', but also noted that 'many accidents have happened to the workmen during the progress of the work, but none fatal'. As an indication of progress being made, he also included in his drawing 'the building on the high ground behind the south front' [i.e. Coates portal] which 'is a public house, built by Lord Bathurst, for the convenience of the workmen employed on the Tunnel and Canal'. When describing the portal itself, he commented that 'there are yet no inscriptions on the tablets on the south front although evidently they are intended to be inscribed'. Was there in fact a plan to complete some form of inscription? If so, it never happened.

1787
John Byng, later fifth Viscount Torrington and a knowledgeable traveller, paid a visit on Wednesday 25 July 1787, when he walked some way beside the canal in the open:

> By a step path I descended on foot, (leaving my chaise near the church) and soon found my way to the intended Saperton navigation; which will join the Severn to the Isis. – A canal has already been dug for seventeen miles, by the side of which I walk'd for some way, and where it cross'd a deep brook several times; then I return'd to the tunnel mouth, at the base of Saperton Hill, which is adorn'd by a Gothic stone front, and whence a sledge cart issued, drawn by two horses, into which I enter'd, (seated on a cross plank) for the pleasure of this inspection.

> Nothing cou'd be more gloomy than thus being dragg'd into the bowels of the earth, rumbling and jumbling thro mud, and over stones, with a small lighted candle in my hand, giving me a sight of the last horse, and sometimes of the arch: and 'Serv'd only to discover sights of woe'. - When the last peep of day light vanish'd, I was enveloped in thick smoke arising from the gunpowder of the miners, at whom, after passing by many labourers who work by small candles, I did at last arrive: they come from the Derbyshire and Cornish mines, are in eternal danger and frequently perish by the falls of earth. - My cart being reladen with stone, I was hoisted thereon, (feeling an inward desire of return,) and had a worse journey back, as I cou'd scarcely keep my seat. – The return of warmth, and happy day light I hail'd with pleasure, having journey'd a mile of darkness.- I next climb'd the hill, with my guide, and was led over the ground I had been under, to several shafts of 85 yards perforation to the tunnel; but unluckily they have not found any ore, etc, to lessen their expence.

I understand that they have made an equal progress (½ mile) at the other end, and hope to meet in 3 years; – when the first passage thro', in a barge, must be glorious and horrid.

[Source: *The Torrington Diaries*: Hon. John Byng, ed. C B Andrews, 1934, vol. 1, 259-60, Eyre & Spottiswoode, London]

1788
Whilst convalescing in Cheltenham in the summer of 1788, George III made visits around the district, hence:

The curiosity of travellers has been much excited; and the numbers of persons who have been to view this work are incredible. When their Majesties were at Cheltenham, they were desirous of seeing the tunnel, and accordingly they visited the entrance under Sapperton hill on Saturday July nineteenth 1788, and expressed the most decided astonishment and commendation at a work of such magnitude, expence, and general utility, being conducted by private persons, undertaken and executed in the compass of seven years.

[Source: *Gentleman's Magazine*, 60 (1790), 388-392]

On the following day, 20 July 1788:

Visit by George III:
They attended him thro' Stroud, where the Royal visitors stopt some time to see the boats pass through the lock. They proceeded to Dudbridge by a new cut, and from thence to Woodchester.

[Source: *Gentleman's Magazine*, 58 (1788), 883]

Traditionally the name King's Reach for the section immediately south-east of the Coates portal is so named after this visit, and it has been associated with the deep cutting down to and beyond Tarlton Road bridge. However, perhaps the name also implies a longer section, extending further along the summit level?

9 Along the Summit to Cirencester

King's Reach to Coates Field

Looking down the canal from the tunnel portal at Coates the cutting stretches away in a straight line to Tarlton Bridge. It is known as the King's Reach following a visit here by King George III in July 1788 when he 'expressed the most decided astonishment and commendation' at the work in progress. The towpath restarts on the right-hand side and remains on this side all the way to Inglesham. Not all of this is accessible, of course. It is only in the cutting that the grandeur of the canal works here can be fully appreciated, with bare rock exposed along the banks. Close to the tunnel entrance is a barge lay-by where boats tied up awaiting their turn to navigate the tunnel. Passage in this direction from east to west was quicker, boosted by the flow of water from the main feeders for the summit level on this side of the tunnel and primarily of course from the Thames Head pumping station. An umbrella of beech trees sheltered the cutting for many years but clearance of dead trees and routine forestry management dramatically opened up the area during 1976. The imagination might be allowed full rein here to visualise the sheer hard work the canal navvies put in to build this section with only hand tools – picks, shovels and wheelbarrows.

Another obvious feature is that throughout the length of this cutting the canal bed is lined with concrete. This was a major area of activity during Gloucestershire County Council's period of restoration from 1900 onwards in the battle against water leakage through fissures in the rock. The concrete lining here was a complete success (it remains so) and the Council even considered such lining for other sections of the canal and even building concrete walls throughout, in order to rid themselves of their greatest problem, but the report in 1909 costing out these options caused consternation and the idea was soon dropped. Nearly a century later, and along this section of the line, it might be recalled that this was the real turning point in the canal's closing years, when the last authority to struggle with the canal's water access and retention problems finally gave up and eventually backed out.

This concreted section down to Tarlton Bridge was cleared out and repaired as one of the early acts of the Cotswold Canals Trust; an access ramp into the canal was provided, the basis for subsequent investigations of the whole tunnel area. At the other end beneath Tarlton Bridge the insertion of stop planks (re-using the original grooves set into the stonework) again serves to hold back a good depth of water which usually flows from the tunnel. This bridge is another fine Thames & Severn structure; what survives today is the rebuild of 1823, kept in good condition as a highway bridge and providing an excellent counter-point to the portal beyond. The canal now swings round to a west/east alignment into a deep cutting; the towpath, however, rises up following the lie of the land here. This section also includes a prominent milestone (*Walbridge 10*), again minus its plate. For the sake of completeness, this is the point to note that four milestone positions (*Walbridge 8* to *Walbridge 9½*) do not exist along the canal line as it has come through the tunnel.

Tarlton Road bridge, rebuilt in stone in 1823 and an impressive counter-point at the end of King's Reach from the Coates tunnel portal.

There remain a number of examples of rock fissures in the canal bed, which could often act as 'blow holes', bursting the clay lining of the bed by water pressure. For this reason a programme of clay re-puddling was carried out along this stretch in 1902-1904. An important part of the water-management arrangements along the summit level were the stop-gates sited at intervals, where a set of grooves in the stonework at a narrowing of the canal bed allowed planks to be inserted in time of emergency to prevent water loss. Single gates were provided at five points along the summit level from the outset to protect this all-important reservoir and so limit losses when leaks developed. The original intention was that these self-acting gates would close off a section when a sudden flow of water occurred. In practice this was not guaranteed (a maintenance problem, again?) and they were replaced by the simple plank-stop, a waisted masonry abutment with a vertical groove for the insertion of a row of planks, stored nearby. Ultimately there were eighteen of these positions along the summit and they can be spotted at strategic points.

Coates roundhouse is a very interesting comparison with the first example seen at Chalford. It has the same dimensions and internal layout, but the roof arrangement is different. Instead of the upright conical shape, the roof here (and at two other roundhouses) was inverted, the whole arrangement concealed behind the circular wall of the building. In such an isolated spot at Coates, this was of course the most successful way of gathering a water supply, piped off the roof into water storage at ground level. Although this building is now derelict (*and dangerous*) the internal layout was recorded some years ago before the roof pattern finally disintegrated. Again, the ground floor began life as a stable with living accommoda-

111

Roundhouses

The five roundhouses of the Thames & Severn are probably its best-known feature, spread out as they are from Chalford through to Inglesham. They were clearly designed and built as a group, completed in 1790-1791, and tend to disguise the fact that other buildings constructed to a more traditional rectangular design also functioned as watchmen's or lengthmen's cottages. However these five occupy visually prominent positions, if to slightly different effect in each case, and a whole study could be made as to who influenced this design and why. Were they round in order to allow the Devil nowhere to hide, as a common story has it? Is a round structure in fact as structurally simple as a rectangular one to build, so in that sense they were not particularly remarkable? Were there parallels available for study in the local Cotswold landscape?

The most obvious variation was the design of the roof. In three cases (Coates, Marston Meysey and Inglesham – all isolated buildings without ready access to water supply), the roof was hidden behind the parapet wall and was inverted (as it still is at Inglesham), so that the roof invert could act as a water catchment area, water being piped off into storage close by. The Chalford and Cerney Wick buildings have a conical roof, almost proudly so, and in each case this is a considerable asset to the building in its location. The choice seems to have been unequivocal.

All five have (or had) the same stucco finish, and were designed with three storeys, the ground floor opening directly at canal level to be used as a stable, with two floors of living accommodation above. Despite subsequent variations over two centuries or more, this arrangement is still apparent. Four of the five still function as homes, Marston Meysey having been rescued from dereliction some years ago. Coates roundhouse, isolated and alone along the towpath from its nearest neighbour at Tunnel House, is now derelict and a sad sight. Last occupied in the 1950s it suffered the inevitable 'closing order' since when its roof was recorded before it collapsed and some protection against decay has been afforded. It still offers something of the sense of isolated responsibility which the canal watchmen must have felt throughout their working lives.

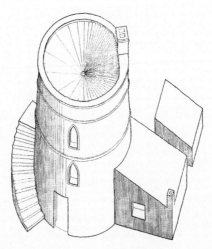

How the inverted roof worked at Coates, draining drinking water off for use. (Illustration courtesy Christopher Powell)

Could this roundhouse in Cirencester Park be a source of encouragement for the canal round-houses? It is half a century earlier and another part of the inspirational landscaping between Earl Bathurst and Alexander Pope which for them included the dream of uniting Thames & Severn within their landscape creation. Or do the wool stoves or teazel towers of the Cotswolds provide another clue, familiar as they must have been to eighteenth century builders? This example at Frogmarsh in Woodchester dates back to the sixteenth century; there was another at Puck Mill. (Photos from postcards, one by W. Dennis Moss, Cirencester)

Coates Roundhouse, still occupied in August 1949. The conversion of the ground floor from stable to living accommodation can be seen, although the first floor entrance remains in use. (Photo courtesy Humphrey Household)

The summit level at Coates roundhouse in 1938, with the railway crossing behind. Shades of Whitworth's 'bad, rocky ground' along here, drawing water away through the fissures in the rock. (Photo Frank Lloyd, courtesy & copyright British Waterways Archives, Gloucester, ref. 5257)

From the survey of the canal undertaken by de Salis in 1896, this view looking west on the summit between Trewsbury and Coates, shows Whitworth's 'bad, rocky ground'. The GWR crosses via the skew bridge in the background. (Photo courtesy Hugh McKnight Collection)

tion above. A scullery addition at the rear in later years indicates a change of use and a greater amount of room for domestic accommodation. Of all the fascinating buildings along the line of the Thames & Severn, this little structure most demands maintenance to prevent further deterioration; some work has been attempted but can nothing further be done?

Just beyond the roundhouse, the canal and towpath pass under a lofty-arched railway bridge, particularly notable for its skew-bridge arrangement, built by the railway engineers when the Swindon to Cheltenham line was being pushed through to Stroud and Gloucester (the line opened in 1845). Well maintained still, it repays study as a remarkable brick construction. The canal summit level is now following the 365ft contour line and here turns into the very upper reaches of the Thames Valley. A straight half-mile stretch leads towards Coatesfield Bridge through a section which although a right of way (and part of the Monarch's Way) can become overgrown in summer. The canal bed remains very dry even in wet weather and this serves to illustrate how bad this section was for water retention. This very stretch was the reason for Robert Whitworth's reference to 'bad rocky ground' when carrying out the original survey.

The bridge is another fine example in stone and here is another significant point on the journey, the furthest point east of the continuous right of way on the towpath (apart from the tunnel) which can be enjoyed all the way up from Stroud. From here the towpath cannot be guaranteed to be a right of way and there will be many examples of the loss of access resulting from the sale of the canal from the 1920s onwards to landowners on either side of the line. Often this division was achieved actually down the centre of the canal bed, in which circumstances it is not surprising that reclamation for agricultural use has sometimes involved the elimination of the towpath. Examples will be found at intervals from here on. From here to the top lock at Siddington the towpath walker will have to resort to alternative footpath routes from time to time.

Thames Head

The sharp turn to the south immediately after Coatesfield (or Trewsbury) Bridge has left its mark on the rubbing stones beneath the bridge arch, where the tow-ropes strained against the bridge as the horse-drawn barges negotiated the bend. From here on the towpath is effectively impassable and *private property*; the route should now follow the signposted footpath off the bridge into the fields. This actually follows parallel to the canal line but at a slightly lower level until it reaches the celebrated source of the river at Thames Head. Despite being dry for much of the year this remains the official source, and was marked until 1974 by the reclining figure of Old Father Thames. This work by Raffaelle Monti was carved in 1851 for the north terrace of the Crystal Palace in London but after the Palace was destroyed by fire it was used elsewhere before being purchased by a member of the Thames Conservancy and re-sited here in 1857. Alas, in such an isolated position, vandalism played its part and the Conservators of the River Thames opted for a safer resting place for this source of inspiration (if not always of water) at St John's Lock on the river at Lechlade. In his place a commemorative plaque (1857-1974) stands beneath an ash tree.

Doubtless this is a big disappointment to many summer visitors but this is a winterwell and the time to appreciate the niceties of the discussion is in mid-winter when the whole of this

A boat-load of Cotswold stone being loaded alongside the quarry at Coatesfield, in this rare view by Cirencester photographer W.H. Monney of Dollar Street, Cirencester, c.1878-1885. The single-storey thatched cottage doesn't look particularly Cotswold; behind, another building is under construction. Compare this with the tumbledown cottage in an earlier view (page 19). (Photo courtesy Corinium Museum Cirencester ref. 1988/162/1)

The first pump at Thames Head was a six-sailed windmill, replaced in 1792 by this Boulton & Watt single-acting beam engine, working a much deeper well, which remained in use until 1854. It is depicted as seen from the road in this view of 1828. Five years later the Stroud engineer John Ferrabee over-hauled the engine in the summer of 1833, and at the same time its long-serving engineer Thomas Toward retired 'after fulfillin' a Sarvitude of 42 years as the local Engineer'.

shallow valley floor regularly floods right across the pasture fields. Nor is this anything new; the county historian Samuel Rudder expressed a clear view in his *New History of Gloucestershire* in 1779:

The head of the Thames or Isis … is commonly reputed to be in this parish; but the well so called does not overflow in the summer, unless in very wet seasons, and there is no constant stream in the place. Indeed if this were perennial, it would not be the highest source of that river …

Up on the left a breach through the canal bank for farm access to Trewsbury *(private property)* once allowed a glimpse of the cottage built in the old Coatesfield quarry here, part of the bed of the canal now being used for a garden. At least one photograph survives to show stone being extracted from this quarry, another example of localised canal-side trading.

Whilst the footpath route across the meadows follows the valley floor, and is indeed now the long-distance Thames Path, the canal remains with the contour line higher up. Before long the A433 road is reached, which is here embanked across the valley floor and follows the line of the Fosse Way south-westwards from the Roman town of Cirencester, a route some 2,000 years old. Alongside the road is the small community at Thames Head wharf, a group of buildings *(private property)* and the surviving bridge, saved because the road was re-aligned here in 1962 so that the old line still crosses the bridge. A plaque inserted on the bridge records all this, but the fast-moving traffic now makes this difficult to appreciate. Thames Head was essentially a roadside wharf, intended to attract traffic from Tetbury and beyond. The wharfhouse was probably built by the mason John Holland in 1784 for the resident agent, a post which only survived until about 1835 when the amount of trade could no longer justify its retention. There was also a small warehouse and some stables.

Although the bridge hole mostly seems to be buried and out of sight, the canal is actually piped beneath the road in a tube. Another sharp turn in the line of the canal takes place immediately after the road crossing, whence the line is contoured around the hillside to the site of the pumping station at Thames Head. Both the driveway along the canal bed and The Pump House now form *a private residence and there is no public access along this section*. In fact, the arrangements as they survive can just as well be appreciated by returning a little way south-west along the road to re-join the Thames Path and thence across the fields once again, towards Kemble.

As the canal, now high up on the embankment to the left, turns due east the enlarged and virtually rebuilt Pump House can be seen, where as recently as 1974 the Thames Head engineman's house had been virtually the only surviving building. Very little now remains to tell the story of the successive pumping arrangements here, as the last engine and boiler houses have been demolished and the open well filled in. The need for pumping into the summit level was obvious to the Canal Company from its early days, the intended supply into the summit from the River Churn at Cirencester being too spasmodic and fraught with difficulties. In 1792, only two years after opening the canal, the company installed a Boulton & Watt beam engine and pump. This was later replaced by a more efficient second-hand Cornish engine and pump in 1854. Both engines pumped water from a large oval well 64ft deep dug into the floor of the valley. There were eventually many underground culverts

Henry Taunt's postcard view of the Cornish engine which replaced the earlier and by then worn-out pump in 1854. This engine was acquired from Wheal Tremar near Liskeard, and was quickly installed so that the pump was out of action for little more than eleven weeks. It made a dramatic improvement to the pumping operation and served for over fifty years.

linked back to this well to maintain a supply. The well never ran dry even when pumped continually in the dry summer months, when up to three million gallons of water could be taken up into the canal per day. The last engine and pump worked up until 1912 by which time navigation in the summit level was all but over, and the engine and pump were finally scrapped in 1941 as part of the war effort.

From here the canal continues to follow the contour winding away to the left to the head of a small side valley which it was able to cross at Smerrill with the minimum of embankment construction. The Thames Path however remains firmly with the line of the river and passes the site of the wind-pump (now gone) at Lyd Well – itself a significant source of water to this area. The bed of the river has deepened steadily and is influenced by the outflow from the four main springs of water. Eventually the A429 Cirencester-Kemble road is reached, where the river goes beneath the road via a fine piece of culverting (put in when the railway was built in 1841). We can now only imagine the full impression of the arrangement when the railway branch line into Cirencester was carried high over both river and road here.

From this point on the A429 the walker must choose to remain with the Thames Path as an alternative route all the way to Cricklade, Inglesham or Lechlade, or seek to pick up the canal line at specific points between here and Siddington, where the towpath can be regained. This Guide assumes the latter course, as it seeks to describe the historic or 'heritage line' of the canal.

Smerrill to Siddington

About half a mile along the road towards Cirencester *(not a recommended walking route)* is the site of Smerrill Aqueduct. To the left, the line of the canal clearly meanders along the contour line. It then turned east where it crossed the road via a single-arched stone aqueduct, all trace of which has long gone. Inevitable as this may have been, such a feature might now be regarded as a heritage asset and worth preserving. However, the stone arch was removed as a road hazard soon after abandonment of this section of the canal in 1927. It was gone by 1931 and some years after that the earthen embankment was itself cut back for road-widening, at which time the profile of the canal cut was clearly seen. However, the earthen embankments survive on either side with dry-stone walling revetments – the whole built by William Mytton, whose Cutting Book records his work for the company over four years of constructing the canal. To the canal cutters, this section was known as Mr Coxe's Barn after the splendid example of a Cotswold stone barn just below the embankment. For some years this was the home of Smerrill Farm Museum, a fine collection of old farming tools and implements, now unfortunately dispersed. It is now refurbished as a B&B. It is possible to park on the old road line where the arch once stood and study the re-shaped embankments on either side. Stop-gates were installed on either side of the aqueduct, and these survived the changeover to plank-stops elsewhere along the summit.

Pursuing the line by road from here on, the side road signposted Ewen and Poole Keynes just past the cottages opposite keeps the canal line in sight (visible as an embankment across the field). After a short distance the Cirencester railway branch line once crossed both road and canal on a three-arched stone structure here. The two arches over the road remain but that over the canal has been underfilled. Just beyond this point can be found what was until recently the remains of an accommodation bridge known as Halfway Bridge, as this is approximately the mid-point between Wallbridge and Inglesham. This has been splendidly rebuilt (datestone 1997) and offers an excellent opportunity to get a feel of coming across these isolated canal bridges out in the countryside. Built largely in brick but with a fine stone arching (and complete with plank-stop) it also has a fine batter in its typical canal-bridge shape, made the more satisfying by the re-creation of steps down and the small Ewen wharf alongside. This was built here or brought into use here to supply not only Ewen but perhaps Kemble too and other local villages.

It is a pleasure to walk the next half-mile section, opened up with the landowner's support as a permissive route. A fine run of dry-stone walling is a reminder of the height which the towpath boundary wall may have been (much of it elsewhere is now considerably reduced). About halfway along is milestone *Walbridge 12 ½*, round-headed and lichen-covered in the bank. This section ends at the site of Park Leaze Bridge, although a further half-mile or so can be followed alongside the Cirencester road, where the towpath also takes on a magical feel through a tree-covered section where the canal is usually in water.

Return to the road is necessary (it can also be followed round from Ewen wharf too) as the journey continues towards Siddington and Cirencester. Along this section between Thames Head and Upper Siddington, the bridge at Halfway is the only one surviving of a total of nine. In fact, for the whole of the eastern section from Coates to Inglesham only

The single-arched masonry structure of Smerrill Aqueduct over the Cirencester to Malmesbury road shows well in this postcard view c.1914, looking towards Kemble. Once the canal had closed in 1927 the removal of this obstruction to traffic increased in priority and it was removed by 1931. (Photo courtesy Humphrey Household)

With the aqueduct removed some thirty years before, further road improvements were made at Smerrill in 1960 by cutting back the embankment and widening the road to create the present alignment. This view looking towards Kemble. (Photo courtesy Corinium Museum Cirencester ref. 1976/479/1)

sixteen of the forty-two bridge crossings (or 38%) remain intact, whereas the western line up to Sapperton from Stroud still has twenty of the original thirty-one remaining (or 65%). This fact alone illustrates the varying fortunes of the two sections of the Thames & Severn.

Further along is the site of Furzenleaze or Level Bridge. Canal line and road part company; a footpath sign directs along the towpath line across a field to the bridge and lengthman's cottage at Bluehouse. An attempt to rationalise this right of way around the road was defeated in 1978 and although short, this is another link preserved in the chain. Actually, the canal was in a cutting here and where in-filling took place it has sunk just enough to be detectable across the field. However there is absolutely no trace of the considerable activity here in 1902–1904 when contractors dug out clay and re-puddled sections of this length. The bridge has been levelled but the lengthman's cottage survives, known as Copsefield and is *private property*. Extensions in recent years are obvious but note particularly the way in which the building was originally constructed into the canal bank.

Beyond Bluehouse, where the garden now occupies the canal bed, there is little of note in the infilled section which follows two large S-bends along the contours and one might wonder whether the canal ever existed. Much of the next mile or so was filled in by Cirencester Urban and Rural District Councils using the length as a town refuse tip for a number of years. Only a slight dip in the fields and (best clue) the hedge lines remain to give any indication on the ground. Some may argue that future restoration along sections such as

Watchman's cottage at Bluehouse, Furzenleaze, on the summit level in 1921. (Photo Frank Lloyd, courtesy & copyright British Waterways Archives, Gloucester, ref. 5276)

this might take a shorter alignment, avoiding some of the more obvious meanderings of the contour line. The route is picked up again at the site of Ewen Road Bridge and across one more field at Minety Road Bridge. Both have now been levelled and indeed were points of access to the refuse tip along this section. From the junction of the Ewen and Minety roads, a left turn and immediately right gives access to Siddington. En route to the village the canal line can be seen over to the right marked by a line of trees. At Upper Siddington, a right turn by the playing fields re-joins the canal at the Siddington flight of locks. This is the point at which to consider the link with Cirencester before continuing along the main line.

The Cirencester Arm

Along the entire length of the Thames & Severn Canal, the short but important branch – or arm in canal terminology – from the junction at Siddington into Cirencester is one of the least well-preserved and has been one of the most ill-treated in terms of conservation. This was perhaps inevitable as the pressures of growth after the Second World War forced the town to develop further to the south and indeed to take advantage of the derelict line of the old canal, much of which is now buried beneath the Love Lane industrial estate. Not surprisingly, this 1 ¼-mile-long arm is not included in plans for restoration, although it is to be hoped that conservation of its line as a linear access into Cirencester will not be further eroded.

Why a branch to Cirencester at all? The answer is at least two-fold, to tap into and develop the trade which the town could contribute to the economy of the canal, and also as a principal access to water supplies, obtainable via various sources into the River Churn. The arm in fact extends the length of the summit level and so too its function as a reservoir, supplying the canal as a whole. Access to enough water, as ever on the Thames & Severn, was always a matter of concern.

Whilst the line of the arm leading off from the junction at Upper Siddington is inaccessible, it can be picked up at the crossing point of the Siddington to Ewen and Kemble road, where there was once a slight rise at the site of Pools Bridge, long since levelled. The next infilled section, although a public footpath, has been overgrown and inaccessible for years but is now under restoration; there is an alternative route via the Pound Close development a little further down the hill, where the footpath regains the towpath at the far end. Just here was the site of a lattice girder bridge providing footpath access to the Old Rectory and the nearby school, which opened in 1860. This bridge was replaced some years ago.

There follows a half-mile section which has not been infilled and still holds water at certain times of the year. Considering the significance of Cirencester in the history of the Thames & Severn, it seems a pity that this sole surviving open section of the arm should remain so neglected and misused. Might it be adopted for some environmental purpose, perhaps? Incidentally, there were no milestones along the arm, and the numbering sequence from Wallbridge doesn't allow for it.

As the industrial buildings of Love Lane are reached, the towpath becomes a footpath, and then a walk along pavements and paths into the town. This is probably the least visually interesting way to approach the town and is something of a labour of love, but it is worth persevering as a wander around Cirencester is well worth the effort. As the towpath reaches the

Not often photographed, the junction at Upper Siddington with the arm to Cirencester off to the left, in 1961. Wharf House is in the background with workshops beyond. (Photo courtesy C.H.A. Townley, Rodborough)

Coal at Cirencester

The wharf at Cirencester was typical of the small-scale venues which provided the primary sources of income for the Canal Company and those who traded along its length. Although other goods were moved across the wharf, both in and out of the town, the import of coal destined for the town's fireplaces was the dominant trade, on which several local businesses concentrated.

Frank Gegg with one of his coal carts and pony Joey on the weighbridge at Cirencester wharf, a typical town carrier's scene. (Photo courtesy Cirencester Archaeological & Historical Society)

Frank Gegg was a coal and coke merchant in Cirencester, trading both from 184 Gloucester Street, where his father Joseph had a grocery business from 1858-1912, and from Canal Wharf. Here he had offices from at least 1894 until 1921 when he packed up, no doubt forced to contribute to the general abandonment of the canal as a means of communication. From 1922 until his death in 1926 he was listed as representative of another Cirencester coal & coke business, S.H. Cole at the railway wharf in Sheep Street, which was effectively just across the road from the canal wharf. Perhaps his finest hour, at least in the columns of the *Wilts & Glos. Standard*, was the arrival of the coal barge *Staunch* in March 1904, heralding the return (albeit short-lived) of coal traffic by canal.

A later scene, probably in the early 1920s when business was running down; Frank Gegg again with Joey alongside the wharf. This is also a fine view of the wharfhouse behind. (Photo courtesy Cirencester Archaeological & Historical Society)

The Gloucestershire County Council records add further information for the period from 1901 until abandonment, during which the local authority owned and ran the canal. Frank Gegg signed a tenant's agreement for his premises at the wharf in October 1907; by 1915 E.R. Cole had a lease there too, to which a cart shed was added in 1917, and S.H. Cole entered a new lease in 1920. With abandonment of the eastern section of the Thames & Severn in 1927, the sell-off began and Cirencester Urban District Council purchased the wharf in that year.

Earlier directories show that Gegg represented the end of a long line of traders based at the canal wharf. *Gell & Bradshaw's Directory* for 1820 records no less than five coal businesses trading in Cirencester, John Brewin in Gosditch Street and four others who each gave their address as 'Wharf' i.e. canal wharf, as this is twenty-one years before the arrival of the railway and its 'wharf': Evans & Chamberlain, William Hill (also in Sheep Street Lane), John Jeffries and Joseph Smith (also in Cecily Hill).

Wharfhouses

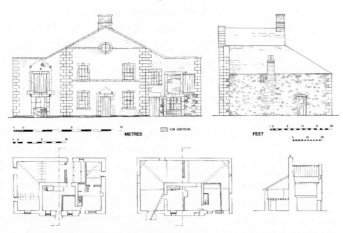

Warehouses are essentially functional buildings, and not necessarily aesthetically pleasing. However, as with other buildings on the Thames & Severn Canal, the three wharfhouses at Cirencester, Cricklade and Kempsford were designed to add some style and perhaps a little elegance to the local canal scene. Construction dates and builders are not confirmed but all three are likely to have been competed in 1789 as they were essential requirements from the outset for successful and secure operation of the canal's business. The wharfman's four-roomed house was wrapped around by the warehousing space, offering security for goods stored there. The rendered façade disguised the rubble stone with which the façade (as well as the remainder of the structure) was built; however, the ashlar quoins remained prominent as did the triangular pediment with its circular window at attic level. In the Cirencester building at least, the living accommodation later spread to one side and an additional doorway was created. All in all, despite the modesty of style, these three buildings represent a brave and pleasing attempt to bring architectural finesse to an essentially functional building.

The wharfhouse at Cirencester Basin photographed shortly before its demolition in October 1975. The infilled Basin is in the foreground. (Photo courtesy Chris Bowler, Cirencester)

buildings, follow the path around to the road and then turn right, heading over the mini-roundabout and straight towards town. At the second mini-roundabout, go straight over and at Bridge End where the road bears left at the garage, go straight over again to find the site of the Chesterton Lane canal bridge. The town's former NAAFI building (now a club) is ahead and all that remains of the bridge is a replacement (and half-hidden) flight of steps down which the towpath can be picked up again.

But before doing so, notice to the right that the old line of Chesterton Lane has been truncated here in creating the town's inner ring road in the mid-1970s. Off to the right again is Bridge Road, which contains one of the few surviving buildings of the canal period (although not a canal building proper), the round-fronted stone building which was the Gas House, built in 1833 and part of Cirencester gas works in the days when supplies were provided locally, in this case by the Cirencester Gas, Gas Light and Coke Co. This building's interesting shape reflects its position squeezed between the road (previously known as Gas Lane) and the line of the canal, which did of course act as a source of supply for coal and other materials. Interestingly this part of Cirencester once had canal and railway cheek by jowl, and much of this evidence has now been erased to improve the road system – evidence of differing transport networks in competition over the years.

Back on the towpath, a short section of track soon comes up against the ring road cutting obliquely across, which must be crossed via the underpass into a housing area. Walking as straight ahead as possible, follow through the garages and houses, where the towpath route has actually survived quite well, although it is a pity that its original function is not recorded in some way, by name or perhaps a plaque. One short section of the boundary wall survives in Rutland Place. Arriving at Querns Road (once called Workhouse Lane – the building is now the Cotswold District Council offices opposite), cross obliquely into Whitworth Road passing the Fosseway Housing offices on the left and follow the line of fir trees at the rear of the houses, which marks the old towpath alignment into the site of Cirencester wharf of which nothing now survives, not even its name. At least the name Whitworth Road recalls canal history. A modern building and yard cover the triangular site in the junction of Querns Road, Querns Lane and the now realigned Querns Hill, the building standing more or less on the site of the wharfhouse. As a terminal basin at the head of the arm, the wharf boasted quite a range of buildings, including a wooden crane, and had access directly onto the road junction.

After its canal days were over in 1927, the whole area passed into the ownership of Cirencester Urban District Council as the town's municipal depot and fire station, where it suffered the wear and tear of such practical uses for over thirty years. A record was made of the largely derelict wharfhouse before its demolition in 1975, a sad loss of one of only three such buildings all to the same design on the Thames & Severn and an important part of its architectural heritage. The other two examples, at Cricklade and at Kempsford, still survive although both now altered and modernised.

The canal basin was lined with stone blocks and formed an impressive structure. Into it from the west side ran two culverts which linked in a series of open leats and culverts for over a mile to the access point with the River Churn at Jenour's Mill or Barton Mill on the western side of Cirencester. The route passed under Cirencester Park and was culverted under the railway yard across the road from the wharf when the railway came to Cirencester in 1841. This source of water was much discussed and argued over. The Act of Parliament in 1783 established the Canal Company's right to the waters of the Churn at Jenour's (Jenner's) Mill and the second Earl Bathurst promised to sell the mill for this purpose. A change of mind in 1785 disrupted negotiations at a time when the Canal Company had begun building and was relying on this source of water as a principal supply for the summit level. Thus committed, the company's men attempted to make the connection, with the result that each party worked to thwart the other's efforts.

It was not until 1791 that an agreement was reached, which allowed the company to have control over the sluice and take water freely when there was a sufficient level for all consumers further down the river; otherwise compensation was payable on an hourly basis to each of the mills concerned. For the nine mills below Jenour's affected in this way, the hourly rate was 6s 5½d, and the average compensation paid out during the period 1796-1835 was about £350pa – a heavy outlay for the company. Even as late as 1904, when only five mills were still in operation, the compensation rate was 3s 6½d per hour. Such was the difficulty of obtaining the canal's essential ingredient.

Although the basin was not filled in for some years after 1927, it seems that blockages in the culverts feeding into the basin and the backing up of water contributed to flooding in parts of the town in 1929. Today, little remains of this culvert system, the victim of the Phoenix Way re-development from the 1970s-1990s in the old railway yards on the west side of the town. Archaeologists (this writer included) have re-discovered the culvert from time to time in the course of pursuing Cirencester's earlier history, for the impressive west gate of the Roman town lay just across the road from the canal wharf. The open section of the leat only finally disappeared when the present Waitrose store was constructed in the mid-1990s. The visitor would be hard pressed to track its line today.

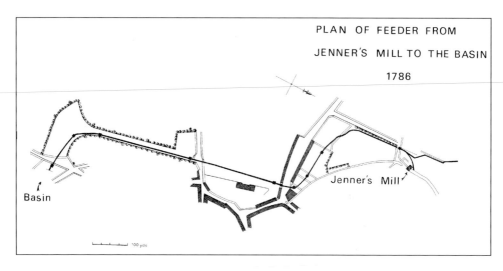

This feeder was partially underground as a culvert and partially an open leat. It crossed beneath the front of Cirencester Park, the home of Earl Bathurst, one of the keenest supporters of the construction of the canal. (Original in Gloucestershire Record Office)

Key Access Points

Tunnel House Inn at *Coates* – see Chapter 8

Thames Head Wharf – Explorer 168 986991
Footpath signposted from busy section of A433; limited parking on old road line. Thames Head Inn just beyond railway bridge. The Thames Path (long distance footpath) runs through this section.

Smerrill – Explorer 168 998989
On A429 Cirencester-Kemble road, with limited off-road parking. Bus services link with Cirencester and with Kemble railway station, a good point of access to this area. The station itself is worth a visit for its historic interest (1882).

Siddington – Explorer 169 030997
Approaching the village from Cirencester, turn first right towards Ewen and Kemble; at Upper Siddington beyond the playing fields turn left to park alongside the lane. The canal bridge at the top of Siddington group of locks is ahead.

Cirencester – Explorer 169 022015
The canal wharf was in the junction of Querns Lane, Querns Road and the old line of Querns Hill. It is best found on foot from the town centre: follow Cricklade Street to the traffic lights, turn right into Querns Lane; at the end, turn left into Querns Road, where the buildings immediately on the right now stand on the old wharf, of which nothing survives.

10 Siddington to Cricklade Wharf

Siddington Locks

The brick bridge at the top of the locks at Siddington is as good a vantage point as any to take in the prospect of the remaining 13½ miles of the eastern section of the Thames & Severn on its journey to the Thames. Here, in the top or Upper Lock just above the bridge, the summit level ends and the long descent begins. The countryside will also be rather different. Progressively there is a feeling of dropping into a larger flood plain, where the scenery is more gentle and inevitably less immediately striking, at least when compared with the steep-sided valleys of the western approaches to the summit level. But this long stretch has its own charm and the next five miles has been opened up as an access route for walkers, if not yet for boaters. The bridge itself is interesting too; it is high and narrow, another brick equivalent of some of the fine stone bridges elsewhere along the line. Still functioning as a highway bridge, it was repaired in 1988 and is well maintained. Look for one small detail: some of the iron clamps holding the coping stones on the bridge parapet are stamped TSC, initials which can also be found on bricks and boundary stones elsewhere.

Looking from the bridge and immediately above the lock, but *not* accessible, is the junction basin of the main line of the canal with the short arm off to the right into Cirencester. Both lock chamber and basin have been cleaned out over the years. On the right and facing the basin with its back to the lane, is Canal House, the former agent's house and an important canal building because here lived the company's representative for this whole section. The workshop for the canal's eastern section was also on this site. Meticulous records kept at this very eastern end of the summit level give a fascinating picture of the trade passing east and west along the canal and indeed also on the Cirencester arm. Not the least useful were the reports back to Brimscombe of the depth of water on the sill of the Siddington top lock; these gave some idea of the levels in the summit so that intending travellers could plan accordingly. These records are preserved along with all the other Canal Company records in the Gloucestershire Record Office and form one of the best collections of records for any single canal in Britain.

The towpath follows down the right-hand side through this closely linked group of locks, all in brick with stone facings. Siddington Second, Third and Lower Locks follow in quick succession, the group of four taking the canal down 39ft from the summit into the long eastern section to the Thames. These are deep locks which remain open and unfenced, and like the rest of the canal should always be treated with respect. Although the lock gates have disappeared, a feature to note is the circular pound above the Second and a widened pound above the Third Lock, to increase the amount of water available in this restricted space for working the flight. The evidence of shortening the locks is also clear. In terms of canal restoration, Siddington is one of the success stories in amenity management. As a first step to winning back the canal from dereliction, work parties from the Trust have cleaned out the whole area and it now presents a charming space, revealing its industrial archaeology interest and at the same time (not always compatible elsewhere) being very much a local amenity as a footpath.

Looking up the locks at Siddington to the upper bridge with Wharf House on the right, c.1902. The canal seems well maintained, reflecting something of the achievements from the period of restoration c.1895 onwards. (Photo courtesy Gloucestershire Record Office)

Between Third and Lower Locks one brick pier survives of the former railway bridge of the Midland & South Western Junction Railway (MSWJR) line from Swindon via Cirencester to Andoversford and the north, opened through here in 1883 and closed completely in 1964. Immediately below is an obvious blockage where the site of the Lower Lock has now disappeared under a modern house (built actually on the lock), its nameplate still preserving the lock name. The towpath is confined between separate housing properties and in retrospect it is difficult to accept that such infilling could have happened so recently, when restoration of the canal was being planned. Since then the line of the canal has become an area of conservation in planning terms, not to be destroyed lightly.

Siddington to South Cerney

At the crossing of the road from Siddington village to Ashton Keynes stood Greyhound Bridge, now levelled but named after the nearby inn. This is a good place to pause for refreshments and indeed the Greyhound must have served a useful purpose for boatmen working down the Siddington flight of locks. It was already in existence when the canal company purchased the land to build the canal. From here for just over a mile the restoration of the

131

Sitting on the beam at Siddington Bottom Lock just before the Second World War. A house now stands on this site. (Photo courtesy David Gardiner, Camborne)

towpath and its return to public use has been another significant achievement in the years since the *Stroudwater & Thames and Severn Canals Towpath Guide* was first published in 1984. At that time, it could be said only that 'from here almost to South Cerney the line of the towpath is virtually impassable and remains on private farmland. The towpath line is actually marked as a public footpath on Ordnance Survey maps, but until such time as the line can be opened up again for public use a return to the car is recommended as far as the lock house at South Cerney'. So thanks are due to all those who have enabled this recreated (and well-maintained) access to be enjoyed once again.

Beyond the crossing route into Plummers Farm, the canal bed continues to hold water fairly well (from the gravel beds beneath) and there is a general encouragement of wildlife. If only for this reason, this is a delightful section to wander along. From this section a good example of a milestone, complete with plate *Walbridge 16 Inglesham 12 ¾,* was recovered in 1971 and generously donated by the landowner to the Corinium Museum in Cirencester for preservation. It can be studied by appointment. For the canal's milestones, see pp.68-69. The isolated and attractive Cowground Bridge has enjoyed Trust-organised restoration, largely of its collapsing arch and side walls; rebuilding the parapet walls remains a task for another day.

Further along, little remains of a swing bridge other than the masonry abutments, and even less of the aqueduct carrying the canal across the River Churn. The river here is quite sizeable and the arch of the aqueduct was the cause of flooding during winter months from the backing up of water – hence its removal. In this section river and canal run close together, the latter on a slight embankment and clear of the problems of flooding. This area was locally known as 'the nooks' – a reference to the winding nature of the Churn, which remains very obvious today. Water management also repays a brief study from the towpath; the water meadows through which the canal was cut may date back to the eighteenth or even seventeenth centuries. This cut required at least one brick-arched culvert created under the canal bed.

From the river through to the South Cerney road, the fields to the south of the canal now form the Claymeadow Rural Interpretation Centre, run by Gloucestershire County Council as a focus for environmental education. The old farm has gone, but waymarked trails offer the chance to experience this 'forgotten' landscape, hemmed in as it must have been for much of its life by both canal and railway. The line of the MSWJR has been running roughly parallel away to the south from Siddington on its route to Cricklade and Swindon. This length of canal also has one of the few surviving milestones along the eastern section (*Walbridge 16½* and complete with OS benchmark) and nearby a welcome modern seat dedicated to the memory of David Fox (1929-1995) a local councillor and keen supporter of the restoration of the Cotswold Canals. A sharp turn on the line takes the canal through the deep Claymeadow cutting (still pleasantly overgrown), its name an indication of ground conditions here. The clay source was turned to advantage in a brick works established on the north side. Its products must at one time have been a regular feature on South Cerney wharf where the cutting opens out and meets the Cirencester-South Cerney road.

Thanks to a substantial towpath clearance project, there is now a choice of footpaths at the approach to the wharf, either straight ahead or by climbing onto the banks of the clay spoil removed from the cutting, which provides a good view of the area. The wharf is now a private house and garden, the latter being cleverly and neatly created from the infilled Upper Lock, the top of three locks here. The coping stones defining the sides of the lock chamber have been retained. South Cerney enjoyed a lock-keeper who was also responsible for the wharf and acted as lengthman. The wharf is actually some little way out from the village but this was not unusual in the canal (and even the railway) period. Its simple character is reminiscent of several others on this canal and an interesting detail of the otherwise simple rectangular lock cottage is a bay-window giving a good view over the lock. In the modernisation of the property this feature has been re-designed. From the wharfside, quantities of coal, timber, stone and agricultural products (as well as the bricks) would have been transported away by farmer's cart and local wagon – this was very much a local canal wharf at the roadside.

South Cerney to Cerney Wick

The road bridge over the canal has long since disappeared. The footpath sign directs the walker obliquely across the fields, sloping gently away to the south east. One might wonder whether the canal ever came this way but following this line it is still possible to make out the sites of the infilled South Cerney Middle and Lower Locks from surviving brickwork and from irregularities in levels; each of the three had a fall of 9ft 4in. Although returned to agricultural use, these locks presumably remain reasonably intact beneath and might again be restored. To the left is South Cerney airfield, now in use by the Army, and one of the many airfields developed in this part of Gloucestershire in the years before the Second World War. It was opened in 1937/1938. The route emerges at an angle onto Northmoor Lane which links the village with the main A419 Cirencester-Swindon road. The bridge here has also been levelled.

The lock and lock house at South Cerney in the early years of the twentieth century.

From here is another delightful section of towpath and canal which can be walked for nearly four miles to Latton Basin, with access maintained over the years by local amenity society and Trust members. The first 1½ miles into the Cotswold Water Park provides a leisurely and still relatively little-known walk of delightful seclusion, hidden from the nearby main roads yet easy of access at either end. The walk is in parts open with views to the level farmland on either side and at intervals shaded in 'groves' of tree growth which delight the eye particularly at high summer. A recently added golf course adds low-key sustainable use. There is relatively little by way of physical remains. At Crane Bridge, the road is now levelled; opposite, the towpath runs along the access track to Crane Farm, rebuilt in recent years from the simple isolated farmhouse in the old water-meadows, which have themselves disappeared as the gravel has been extracted. Along the track about half way to the farm gate is the site of a milestone which until relatively recently still displayed its plate *Walbridge 17½ Inglesham 11¼*, one of the very few still retaining its original mileplate in situ. It was there in 1984 but alas has since disappeared. The removal and loss of such community heritage assets is to be deplored.

Shortly afterwards on the left is Boxwell Spring Lock, which makes its own particular contribution to the history of the Thames & Severn. Also known as Shallow or Little Lock, it has a fall of only 3ft 6in which makes it – apart from the lower chamber at Dudgrove – the shallowest lock on the entire length. In fact Boxwell is an after-thought resulting from a miscalculation of the canal levels and water supplies here, and it was inserted to lower the level of the canal bed in order to channel in water from the Boxwell springs nearby. Supplies were much needed along this stretch to meet the demands of the deep locks at Wilmoreway. Only one of the group of springs could thus be tapped as the southern group, although more prolific, even with these alterations proved to be too far below the level of the canal. The new lock was built in 1792 by the mason and contractor Thomas Cook, for which he was paid

£86 14s 6d. It is interesting to note that Boxwell is a stone-lined lock in comparison with the heavy use of brick elsewhere on this section. Boxwell is also remarkable for its restoration – another self-contained campaign by the Trust, from 1992-1995, which has brought this interesting structure with its fine spill-weir back to life.

From the entrance to Crane Farm the towpath soon reverts to a footpath. The site of the spring is in a small withy bed on the opposite side; in the field behind there used to be a derelict wind-pump, another sign of tapping this resource. Down to the right and at a lower level are the more prolific southern springs, access to which proved difficult to achieve. The towpath shows all the signs of good maintenance, with towpath clearance all along the line plus work on the more difficult tasks of lock repair and reconstruction. The lakes of the Cotswold Water Park are prominent throughout this section. Now Britain's largest water park, its 132 lakes created by gravel extraction cover over thirty square miles. The Park has developed by identifying particular uses for each of the gravel pits as they are worked out, so that water sports, nature conservation and a range of amenity activities are not in conflict. This process continues as gravel is still being worked. The line of the canal offers an important linear amenity route through the northern part of this western section of the Park.

Typical of the eastern section of the Thames & Severn, this view looking towards Crane Bridge at South Cerney was taken by Humphrey Household on 8 April 1947. (Photo courtesy Humphrey Household)

The Lower Lock and cottage at Wilmoreway in the early years of the twentieth century.

Winter scene with plenty of water at Cerney Wick lock c.1900. The upper lock gates look in good order and this view reflects some of the achievements of restoration early in the twentieth century. (Photo courtesy South Cerney Trust)

Cerney Wick lock in dereliction with the charming roundhouse behind, in a view dating from 18 August 1947. (Photo courtesy Humphrey Household)

Although the modern spelling is Wildmoorway, the version preferred in the Thames & Severn Co. records was Wilmoreway, possibly phonetic, or simply Humpback, a word which accurately describes many of the canal's bridges. Just before Wilmoreway Upper (or Humpback) Lock, a line of trees shades the towpath in a most attractive manner. The lock has been cleared of debris and undergrowth revealing once again the mixture of brick and stone in the chamber, testimony to many repairs. Also worth studying is the large overflow weir on the offside of the towpath. In the next stretch, not much survives of the demolished Humpback Bridge, an isolated accommodation bridge between fields, and the next feature of note is Wilmoreway Lower Lock which had a fall of 11ft producing a combined fall of 18ft 6in for these last two locks, thus creating considerable problems of water supply. One part of the solution to this problem can be seen off the towpath alongside the lock. A large stone-lined side pond was built here in 1831, and it is the only example on the eastern section of the canal. Its workings are unusual and rare; the pond was linked to the lock chamber by a large cast iron pipe so that by manipulation of the sluices about two-fifths of the water used in the lock could be drawn off for re-use. The pipe and cast iron lid can be seen clearly in the lock chamber, and in the corner of the side pond the access was until recent years also covered by a cast iron lid. The side pond has been partially re-excavated so that its shape is clear.

The toll cottage and junction lock at Latton Basin, seen here in 1896. Small hayricks stand alongside the junction with the North Wilts Canal. (Photo courtesy Hugh McKnight Collection)

The other precaution taken to control water usage was the building of a lengthman's cottage alongside the lock to ensure supervision of this operation. The lock-keeper moved here from Cerney Wick in 1831, but unlike that roundhouse very little of this building remains. Only part of one wall of the cottage now stands and despite numerous applications to the local planning authority to rebuild the cottage, it remains a ruin, isolated in the countryside. Wilmoreway Lower Lock and its accompanying brick bridge were the subject of a large-scale 'Dig Deep' working party blitz in 1995; the bridge looks almost new (complete with 1996 datestone) and the lock is one of the best examples on the Cotswold Canals of careful reconstruction.

A footpath offers an alternative walk for 1½ miles into South Cerney along the old Wildmoorway Lane. Below the lock and bridge there is a short but attractive section of canal bed often in water; hidden in the bushes on what remains of the towpath is a broken section of a milestone (*Walbridge 18 ½*), just before the tranquillity of the last few miles is returned to reality for the crossing of the Spine Road. This is the key access route into the Cotswold Water Park and the visitor information point, with car park and toilets, is conveniently just across the road. A display panel gives a brief history of the canal with special reference to the section between South Cerney and Cerney Wick. Here the canal enters the county of Wiltshire where it remains for about six miles before coming back into Gloucestershire near Blackgore Bridge above Kempsford.

The public footpath signs direct back onto the towpath and there follows another section opened up in recent years. Unfortunately for most of this next section to Cricklade the traffic noise from the nearby A419 intrudes upon the tranquillity of the walk, and the line of the towpath is rather broken up by landscaping associated with the extraction of gravel on either side and the unfortunate introduction of overhead lines at intervals. However it remains a through route, which also includes another milestone, round-headed, lichen-covered and hiding in the undergrowth (*Walbridge 19*) and complete with OS benchmark. Until recently the local landmark, the tall white chimney of Latton Creamery, survived as an indication of the dairying tradition of farming through which the canal passes for most of its length along the eastern section. Reed beds in the canal are prominent in some places, and the vigorous spread of the colourful but invasive Himalayan balsam and butterbur in others, especially along the approach to Cerney Wick. Not so many years ago, this section was lined with elm trees, another almost forgotten feature of the landscape.

The roundhouse at Cerney Wick, the third of the five examples along the Thames & Severn, remains one of the canal's most attractive buildings and arguably on the canal system as a whole. It is remarkably well preserved and well looked after by its present owners. The original layout can still be appreciated with a stable on the ground floor, a living room entered directly from external steps to the first floor and bedroom(s) on the upper floor. The stone structure remains faced with stucco which together with the narrow gothic style windows and conical slate roof are the building's now familiar characteristics. Alterations over the years have preserved the circular shape and a good touch is the stone ball-finial on top of the roof. The roundhouse, together with its garden alongside the lock and extending into the canal bed, is *private property* and should be respected. Indeed both the house and its setting can best be appreciated from the towpath side. The whole area is indeed a lucky survivor, for the lengthman based here was moved up to Wilmoreway when that cottage was built in 1831 and the Cerney Wick roundhouse was no longer required. It passed out of canal ownership but in spite of that has stood the test of time rather better than its replacement.

Cerney Wick Lock, with a fall of 6ft, is another lock where Trust working parties have been busy over a number of years; the campaign here dredged the lock, repaired its structure (an interesting mixture of stone, red brick and blue brick) and installed new top gates. The mason John Nock, whose men built so much of the canal, was paid £113 for building this lock and he also built the next two locks down at Latton and Eisey. The bridge over the tail of the lock has been levelled. Close by, the Crown Inn is another good stopping place for refreshments.

Cerney Wick to Cricklade Wharf

The next section to Latton is through farmland and is relatively featureless, although no less interesting. There are two milestones, both flat-topped (*Walbridge 19 ½* and *Walbridge 20*), the latter close to the Basin at Latton, in an area where the canal was never puddled with clay as it was cut through the water-bearing gravel which lies just below the whole area here. After half a mile, it is possible to make out in the field what little remains of the T-junction between the 'main line' of the Thames & Severn and its link into the North Wilts Canal, off to the right. There were two bridges in close proximity, one on each route and very little remains

Henry Rodolph de Salis' boat Dragonfly *in Latton Basin during his inspection tour of the canals in 1896.* (Photo courtesy Hugh McKnight Collection)

visible of either, although both bridges are believed to be buried – the top of the abutment walls of the bridge into the basin can still be seen on the ground. Although now overgrown, the large rectangular stone-lined Latton Basin remains a surprise. Its walls survive virtually intact except on the north side where the link with the canal by aqueduct across the River Churn has been severed, a pity as this plus bridges and towpath once formed a most interesting and isolated canal junction. Now the uninterrupted flow of the river makes the basin look like some gigantic error of judgement! At the far end of the basin was the entrance into the North Wilts Canal and alongside it the brick toll cottage. 'Largely derelict and unsafe' at the time when the Towpath Guide was compiled some twenty years ago, it survives albeit largely rebuilt and remains *private property.*

Much of the North Wilts Canal from this point is impassable and not a right of way, although much work has already been done in the growing campaign for the restoration of both North Wilts and Wilts & Berks Canals, which will add to the overall restoration network. Latton Basin was formed in 1819 as part of a typical canal enterprise: the linking of two canal routes for the mutual benefit of both concerns. In fact the short length of the North Wilts Canal (nine miles) linked the Thames & Severn with the Wilts & Berks Canal at Swindon and thus gave an alternative and easier access to the Thames at Abingdon. The upper reaches of the Thames to Lechlade proved a problem for navigation throughout much of the life of the Thames & Severn, so much so that the proprietors were prepared to agree to, and pay for, the development at Latton knowing that this link would cut out the remainder of their own canal between Latton and Lechlade. This new route was inextricably tied up with the fortunes of the Wilts & Berks Canal which by 1906 had incurred such losses that it was forced to close. The lock from Latton Basin into the North Wilts is in fact not a true lock, but a pair of double stop-gates, one controlled by each company and indicative of the importance of water supply to each. The inevitable disputes arose about water levels, leading to argument and misuse, when the gates would be held shut by one party against traffic from the other.

From the levelled (or buried?) site of Weymoor Bridge just to the east of the basin, the changes in access resulting from the construction of the Latton (and Cricklade) by-pass, which is all part of the A419 improvements, become very apparent and have affected the final stages of this section through to Cricklade wharf. The old track from Latton Basin into Latton itself is now a road with a bridge all to itself, and offers one way to return to the old road at Street Farm which is virtually the last house on the Cirencester side of Latton. Continuing eastwards, the line of the canal across the meadows is but a depression in the field, here close to the line of the River Thames itself. It can be followed across to Court Farm, but it might be quicker to follow the new side road which runs parallel to the dual carriageway and passes Court Farm to reach the road into Cricklade at Cricklade Wharf. This road passes the former Latton Mill. This section of canal line is bedevilled by changes to road alignment, and so the eye of faith is required to picture its former route, all now infilled and effectively destroyed by the new road, including the former site of Latton Bridge where the canal crossed under the old line of the road and where the Latton culvert is now inserted. Not surprisingly, this was one of the first levelling operations following the canal's abandonment, its site is actually just beyond the last two cottages on the old alignment; the remains of the turning basin now form part of the cottage gardens. Thereafter, for the short stretch to the wharf the line of the canal is mirrored by that of the dual carriageway, and the wharf building will soon be apparent to the south of the road. Midway along stood Latton Lock with a fall of 9ft 4in. It too has vanished completely.

Cricklade Wharf is on the left of this painting c.1920, looking west to Fairford Lane Bridge. Hayricks stand on the wharf. (Photo courtesy Cricklade Museum, copy in Corinium Museum Cirencester ref. 1987/262/3)

Humphrey Household's charming mid-summer studies of the wharfhouse and farm at Cricklade, in August 1949 and 1947 respectively. Despite alterations, the façade remains largely intact, and the rear elevation reveals the functional storage nature of the building. (Photos courtesy Humphrey Household)

Approaching Cricklade (although the Thames & Severn itself never entered the town) the most outstanding feature is Cricklade Wharf, one of the two preserved of the three examples of this particular design, and despite the traffic now the better situated for external study from both front and rear. The building, now Wharf Farm and *private property*, is another example of a refurbished canal building; it has been re-roofed and its façade maintained and re-decorated, so that the building has an impact when seen, as most people do see it, from the dual carriageway immediately across the field. This wharfhouse or warehouse, as at Cirencester and Kempsford, had at least two functions; firstly, as accommodation for the wharfinger in the central part of the building and secondly as storage space for goods on either side and to the rear of the living accommodation, all under the one large roof. Despite later alterations, the doorway access points for goods on the ground floor and first floor of each wing survive, and even without the hoists over these doorways this gives an excellent impression of the way the building was used. In plan it follows the Cirencester example very closely. Of all the other features of the wharf, small stables still survive, although other buildings on the other side of the wharf have gone, and the old diamond-shaped basin has been filled in and now forms a paddock in front of the buildings.

Key Access Points

Siddington – see Chapter 9

South Cerney Wharf – Explorer 169 047982
Alongside the Cirencester to South Cerney road via Preston toll-bar; very limited roadside parking. The wharf building and grounds are *private* – a footpath gives access to the canal line.

South Cerney – Explorer 169 049970 (village cross-roads)
No roadside parking at Northmoor Lane. Instead park considerately in the village, and walk along the delightfully named Bow-Wow to reach the site of Crane Bridge. A longer walk leaves the end of Station Road at the eastern end of the village and follows the Wildmoorway Lane to the locks of the same name.

Cotswold Water Park – Spine Road Information Point at Explorer 169 072971
Good access, car parking and toilets make this site an excellent point from which to explore the whole eastern section of the canal between South Cerney and Cricklade; from the A419 Cirencester-Swindon road take the Spine Road Junction exit and over the roundabout(s) follow the brown Cotswold Water Park signs for a short distance along the Spine Road.

Cerney Wick – Explorer 169 079960
Limited parking at roadside and close access to the Crown Inn.

Cricklade Wharf – Explorer 169 099945
Access into the centre of Cricklade, then take the old Cirencester road to the north. After about ½ mile, the wharf is on the right, just beyond the footpath entry into North Meadow, and before the road joins the dual carriageway. Limited roadside parking.

11 Eastern Section to the Thames

Cricklade Wharf to Eisey

Construction of the A419 dual carriageway has created a number of obstructions to the canal, the most obvious being the physical barrier it represents to continuing along the canal's historic line. But there has also been the psychological barrier created by the threatened destruction of the plans for restoration. In fact, a significant battle was fought out on this Latton by-pass (as it was known at the time) and – followed by other similar battles elsewhere in the country against new roads cutting the canal line for good – has resulted in government policy being changed so that lines of potential restoration should not be severed in this way. The story of the Latton culvert on the site of Latton Bridge is therefore of more than local interest.

The fact remains that a short section of the journey along the canal line is rendered pretty unpleasant by constant traffic noise, offset by the provision of a footpath route over the new road. Picking up the line in the truncated section of old road alongside Cricklade canal wharf at Wharf Farm, nothing now remains of the canal bridge at this point, but a new path immediately alongside the dual carriageway takes the route around to the foot of the overbridge. At this point and beneath the bridge, it is possible to appreciate another inserted stormwater culvert passing obliquely under the road immediately underneath the bridge. The path swings up and over the new bridge and comes down to join the towpath line where the still-overgrown line of the canal can be detected heading off towards Eisey. Although a right of way and despite being thoroughly cleared in recent years, this next section remains heavily overgrown with a great deal of thorn hedging, and effectively marks the eastern end of the easily-accessible towpath, which has been followed all the way from Siddington. Perhaps the remarks made in the *Towpath Guide* at Siddington (see p.132) about looking forward to restoration of the towpath might be repeated here for the next stage of activity?

The remainder of the towpath from here to Inglesham is almost completely inaccessible, there are no rights of way along it, and some landowners are understandably reluctant to allow free access across their land. Opening up this whole area in some suitable, sympathetic and mutually agreed way remains one of the next major challenges to restoration, bearing in mind that one of the four principal aims of the Cotswold Canals Trust is 'to promote the use of all the towpath as the Thames & Severn Way long distance path'. The alternative Thames Path, further to the south through most of this area, is no substitute for recreation of this historic canal line, although its route can be accessed from here by returning into Cricklade.

Access by car is the only practical way to study what survives of the 6½ mile section from Eisey to Inglesham. The minor (although busy) road to Kempsford and Whelford provides the best access and a turn off after half-mile signposted Eisey (or Eysey) provides access down the approach road (another half-mile) to Eisey Manor Farm. The canal bridge just before the farm has been levelled and the canal route to either side of it is very overgrown. Although *private property*, limited parking is possible for exploration of the two most striking features, a pair of complete milestones removed here from their original positions further down the canal, because of which both have survived in good condition. They are round-headed examples *Walbridge 22 Inglesham 6 ¾* and *Walbridge 22 ½ Inglesham 6 ¼*.

Inaccessible on *private property* further east along the canal line is what remains of the lock and lock cottage at Eisey, the rectangular cottage now largely derelict, although less so than its contemporary at Wilmoreway. Both were built in 1831 to house lengthmen redeployed along there respective lengths, the man here being moved up from Marston Meysey. The cottage seems small but inside was a two-up, two-down arrangement; in the basement, built into the canal bank were two stable/storage rooms reached by an outside door. Of all the isolated buildings along the canal this must have been one of the most isolated, reached only by boat or a walk along the towpath.

Eisey to Marston Meysey

Following the road towards Kempsford, the canal line is off to the south; Rucks Bridge, minus its parapets, survives in good condition and is another example of a red-brick accommodation bridge out in the fields. The next point at which contact with the canal line can be made is at Marston Meysey Wharf where the fourth of the group of five roundhouses survives. Not actually in the village of Marston Meysey itself, the site of the wharf is down a

Eisey cottage, like its twin at Wilmoreway, was isolated along the towpath. Both date from 1831. In this view of 1896, the scene is one of undisturbed calm. (Photo courtesy Hugh McKnight Collection)

In 1961 the roundhouse at Marston Meysey stood isolated and decaying alongside its bridge. The stucco remained and the function and design of the three-storey building exactly mirrored its companions at Coates and Inglesham. (Photo courtesy C.H.A. Townley, Rodborough)

farm track alongside farm buildings; this is a public right of way to Castle Eaton, although the old line over the surviving canal bridge has been diverted around the extensive refurbishment which has brought new life to the old roundhouse and its well-preserved bridge alongside. *This is private property viewable from the footpath only.* This was once a tiny country wharf and today it is very difficult to appreciate the optimism of the canal proprietors in establishing such remote wharves; however, each was intended to serve the local community over a widely scattered rural area which was itself equally remote from any alternative and reliable transport system.

The bridge is a splendid survival, now unused and almost intact in red brick with a grand shape and still retaining its coping. The wharf is largely obliterated. For many years the roundhouse was allowed to become increasingly derelict. It now once again has a new life, its shape preserved by the careful addition of new buildings alongside, to make an unusual home. The exterior finish reflects the original render and the overall shape of the roundhouse has not been broken. This was one of the buildings with the inverted conical roof design, intended as water catchment in this isolated spot (see pp.112-114).

To either side the canal has been filled in and it is easy to see how complete has been the return to agriculture of this part of the eastern section. There is hardly a depression in the ground or a different colouration in the cultivated soil to mark the canal route. The next two small roads through to Castle Eaton crossed over the canal via Crooked Bridge and Blackgore Bridge respectively, both of which were levelled many years ago. Only the occasional presence of red bricks in the hedgerows and a small rise in the road levels reveal where they used to be. However, Oatlands Bridge does survive, in splendid isolation just in the fields opposite the Dunfield turning, and was not levelled because of the wishes of the owner some years ago. Discovering it by chance must raise all sorts of questions for anybody unaware that a canal once passed this way. At least one brick stamped 'Stonehouse Brick & Tile Co. Ltd' can be found built into the parapet, an indication of materials being brought up the canal from elsewhere along the line, perhaps in this case for repairs or rebuilding. Once again, on either side the canal bed has been filled in and imagination is now required to recall the canal scene.

Kempsford

Through the village, the canal line follows to the south of the main village street and is inaccessible behind the houses. Along here was the site of one of the Thames & Severn swing bridges, a rather grand example behind the Green, giving access to the land between the canal and the River Thames. Just past the George Inn a short lane off to the right is called Wharf Lane, a clue to what survives beyond the row of red brick cottages. Kempsford Wharf stands with its back to the road, facing down to the canal. Until the death of its long-time occupant

The wharfhouse at Kempsford, photographed by Arthur Watts in August 1969. (Photo courtesy & copyright British Waterways Archives, Gloucester, ref. 1205.5)

Dudgrove double lock in 1814 as published in The Thames 1811-22 *by W.B. Cooke, with a barge in the top lock. The combined drop of 11ft 6in made the middle gates look impressively high, the design of which can be appreciated.*

Looking into Dudgrove double lock from the east, a view recorded as part of de Salis' survey of the canals in 1896. (Photo courtesy Hugh McKnight Collection)

Grace Walker in 1998, it remained much as it must always have seemed, an interesting example of the Thames & Severn style of wharfhouses (the third in the sequence from west to east), little changed internally as well as externally from its working days. To the same design as Cirencester and Cricklade and serving the same purpose, it is however a narrower building. Beyond the entrance pillars with a pair of old wooden gates and at an angle to the lane lay the wharf area, still with what remained of the ticket office, stables and various cart and storage sheds. Immediately beside the entrance to the small whitewashed cottage was the 'beer house' for the wharf, serving its beer through a hatch between the buildings. Gentle decay was the order of the day, allowing the warehouse to be properly recorded by English Heritage before changes and improvements could take place. The *Towpath Guide* noted that 'externally it survives almost untouched and well deserves to be preserved for its history alone.' Well, now it has and the Wharf House once again has a real sense of place, fully refurbished as a home; the whole area remains *private property with no right of access*, although it can be glimpsed from Wharf Lane.

Immediately east of the wharf and now infilled was the Whelford feeder, supplying water for this canal section down to Inglesham; supplies were taken from the outflow at Whelford Mill, the last mill on the River Coln about two miles away. The feeder made its way across the flat land of the Thames Valley and with only a small drop in level needed constant clearing out to maintain the flow. It proved to be a very valuable feeder supplying the five-mile pound between Eisey and Inglesham, which included Double Lock at Dudgrove and the junction into the Thames, a combined fall of almost 18ft. The line of the feeder can be followed, where its route ran in front of the houses on the left approaching Whelford from Kempsford. The course has mainly been filled in but further along the road at Popes Corner the feeder ditch is still open but carries no water now. It follows round a bend in the road to cross under it just before Whelford Mill. By looking down into the river from the bridge here the arch taking the feeder out of the mill race can be seen in the wall of the house.

Kempsford to Inglesham

From Kempsford wharf the canal curved to the humped-back Kempsford Bridge, now levelled to make traffic flow easier through the village, and from here the route crosses open countryside devoid of houses until it joins the Thames three miles away. In the village the canal and Thames are only a hundred yards apart and many proposals were put forward suggesting a linkage into the Thames either here or at Dudgrove; all of them were shelved. From Kempsford Bridge the canal route is *strictly private property with no access* and indeed with little to see. Green Lane Bridge, down a track a little way beyond Kempsford, is another levelled bridge site. Hedge lines remain one of the few clues of alignment on the ground; the line swings north-east to pass Brazen Church Hill, isolated some 300ft high, but even then it has to enter a deep cutting into which it has been tiered down as it approaches the half-collapsed Hamfield Bridge. Wildlife flourishes along these reaches, which seem to hold water fairly well, probably due to the clayey soil through which the line is cut. A more understandable reason for the wildlife is the complete lack of human intrusion.

The only farm is at Dudgrove, its long access road signposted 'Dudgrove Only' from the

Inglesham roundhouse, bridge and lock, the classic Thames & Severn group, seen here when the canal looks to be in reasonable condition.

road north of Whelford. By following this road until it comes into the yard of Dudgrove Farm, it is possible *strictly with permission* to walk down the track to the site of Dudgrove Bridge, now levelled for agricultural access. Above this bridge the canal line survives from Hamfield Bridge to the west although now very overgrown. From Dudgrove Bridge it is possible to turn left along a track alongside the canal, which soon ends just short of Dudgrove Double Lock. *Permission to visit this isolated and dangerous spot must be obtained from Dudgrove Farm.* The milestone just above the locks survives; its plate *Walbridge 28 Inglesham ¾* is now on display in the National Waterways Museum in Gloucester.

Dudgrove Double Lock is the only example of its type on the whole length of the Thames & Severn. The upper chamber is a normal red brick deep lock with a 9ft fall and typical of so many locks along the line. However, it leads directly into a roughly-built lower chamber constructed of loose stone walling with only a 2ft 6in fall. The story behind this is an interesting one. The canal had been built this far by the early months of 1789 but this final section to join the Thames had yet to be agreed or even marked out on the ground. The cause of the dispute was the state of the upper reaches of the river, a notoriously ill-kept section and difficult for navigation. Fearful of achieving so much and then running into problems of this kind, the canal proprietors sought alternative solutions, including even a direct cut from Dudgrove to Abingdon, which in fact anticipated the solution later offered to this same problem by the alternative North Wilts Canal and Wilts & Berks Canal routes to Abingdon, and helps to explain the willingness of the Thames & Severn authorities to dispense so readily

The Inglesham group seen from the River Thames, another classic view. Here is the junction, the Thames off to the left under the footbridge, the Coln off to the right and the canal under the bridge. (Original photograph W. Dennis Moss of Cirencester)

with the whole of this eastern section in due course. But the problem in the year in which the canal was opened was indeed a pressing one, and the only solution was to cut the originally approved line to join the river at Inglesham. This meant that at Dudgrove a further fall was required, hence the afterthought which the lower lock represents. The nature of its construction also suggests that perhaps hopes lingered for a better solution and a new line in due course.

At this point the river is very close and remains so as far as Inglesham. The actual point of contact with the river was also under discussion; a junction at Inglesham avoided the shallow stretches known to exist immediately above, and was also of course the junction of the Rivers Coln and Thames, thus ensuring deeper water. At Dudgrove, remains of the upper chamber still include the bottom pair of gates, almost closed, but they are very decayed and the balance beams have collapsed onto the lockside. In the lower chamber the rough unmortared sloping sides are in complete contrast to any other lock masonry along the canal; again the bottom gates are still in position but very decayed. Having explored these two locks a return up the track to Dudgrove Farm is now necessary, leaving the canal heading off to the north-east where it is crossed by a farm access track and also by a drainage ditch cut completely through the canal bed. This length remains full of reeds and the towpath is impassable.

Parkend wharf at Lechlade, originally an eighteenth century barge master's house, purchased and altered by the Canal Company in 1813. In this post-war view, the car stands close to the weighbridge. (Photo courtesy Cotswold Canals Trust)

Inglesham and Lechlade

At Inglesham the canal finally reached the Thames, but its story is also inextricably tied up with the commercial life of nearby Lechlade, the long-established town on the river just a mile or so below the junction. The two should be studied together, and they make a whole in terms of canal and river navigation.

From the Market Place in the centre of Lechlade, there is a short walk to the riverside along Thames Street, the main A361 road to Swindon, and so on to Halfpenny Bridge over the river where it is possible to survey the river scene and the area of wharfage immediately upstream. Access to the towpath on the southern side is the best and safest point of study. Lechlade belongs to the river, and its history is very much bound up with serving the river trade in all its forms over centuries. Today this is all leisure activity, thankfully still rather restrained, but evidence of earlier commercial activity can be detected. Seen from across the river, the range of buildings includes the recent refurbishment of a fine old warehouse, now known to be a rare purpose-built timber-framed warehouse of the seventeenth century on the town's Free Wharf.

Alongside is Parkend Wharf and together these provide the focus for most riverside activities today. Parkend was acquired by the Canal Company in 1813 to replace its arrangements at Inglesham. The name may have links with the opening of the canal too, by an association with a colliery of the same name in the Forest of Dean. Parkend Wharf was at that time occupied by Richard Gearing, followed by Cirencester merchant William Hill early in the nineteenth century, until the Canal Company acquired it. In so doing it joined a long tradition of riverside boat-owners and traders at Lechlade. A warehouse and the company agent's house survive, one now a public house and the other used as flats. Access to the wharf either from Thames Street or more picturesquely from Bell Lane allows this area to be studied in detail. On the waterside, the stone edging to the wharf can be seen, although one must imagine the barges tied up to unload coal, stone and agricultural products and take on new orders.

Although Inglesham can be accessed on foot by road (some public, some private) from the Cirencester road out of Lechlade, the most pleasant route to Inglesham is along the riverside by the southern bank, where a walk across the fields soon brings the roundhouse and warehouse in sight, surrounded by trees and occupying a delightful position where the canal and the River Coln enter the Thames. Via an overbridge the path crosses over and allows closer views of the roundhouse *(private property)*. This is the fifth in the sequence, and the third example of an inverted conical roof. Until 1996, the roundhouse had one tenant for nearly fifty years and it has remained largely unmodernised. The warehouse alongside provided the same storage and security of goods in transit as similar buildings at other wharves along the canal also offered; many of those were in similarly isolated spots. This little group is alongside Inglesham Lock and just beyond was the terminal basin, which was also used as a turning pound for barges. Inglesham Lock with a 6ft fall brings the canal down to the level of the Thames and remains in good condition as does the bridge over the tail of the lock (both built in stone). The bridge bears the date 14 November 1789, just five days before the first boat passed through the canal and into the Thames.

The final milestone, complete with its plate, was moved off the towpath into the garden of the roundhouse some years ago. It records *Walbridge 28½ Inglesham ¼* and remains well known if only because Humphrey Household's study includes his excellent photograph of it. It also serves as a reminder that, with the addition of the 1¼ mile arm to Cirencester, the total journey is some thirty miles from Stroud, to which should be added the additional seven–plus miles of the Stroudwater to complete the entire journey from Severn to Thames. With the remainder of the river itself beckoning another journey (and the Thames Path easily accessible to do so), now is a good time to recall Temple Thurston's *The Flower of Gloster* story, where Eynsham Harry took his farewell of 'that writer chap from London', then 'turned the barge around in Inglesham Basin' and set off on his homeward journey back to the Midlands through the 'water-roads of England'. In this particular spot on a sunny summer's afternoon, with little stirring in the breeze, it might all seem just like yesterday, as the author surely intended.

Key Access Points

Cricklade Wharf – see Chapter 10
Lechlade – Explorer 170 207997
There are several car parks in the town centre, plus a good choice of refreshments and accommodation. Parking on Parkend Wharf is for patrons only. The route to Inglesham from the A417 Cirencester road is via an 'Unsuitable for Motor Vehicles' lane, which in fact makes an enjoyable circular walk from Lechlade, returning back along the river.

Families of the canal

The 1881 Census returns provide a snapshot of some of the Canal Company's staff who were living along the line at that time. At the Coates roundhouse is George Smith aged thirty and described as 'summit watchman'; with him are his wife Sarah and three young children. Nearby, living in one of the cottages at Thames Head is Albert Sparrow, aged forty-three, with his wife and three children; he is described as 'engine driver on the canal'. At Blue House is William Skinner, also in his forties, who is a 'canal labourer', and at Siddington is William Pratt, 'Superintendent of Thames & Severn Canal', living at the Wharf with his wife and daughter. Up the arm at Cirencester wharf is William Sharp, aged seventy-three and born in Minchinhampton, who is the 'wharfinger'.

Interestingly, there are three boats moored up at Siddington at the time of the census, alas un-named. John Gleed aged forty-six and born in South Cerney is 'captain' of one; Henry Crook aged eighteen and born in Chalford has another, and the third is in the charge of William Phipp, aged forty-eight and born in Lechlade, the only one of the three who has a mate with him, Henry Bennett, an eighteen-year-old born in Ebley. Phipp is the same surname as that of Henry, the 'coal merchant and wharfinger' at Kempsford, whilst the roundhouse at nearby Marston Meysey had by this date gone out of canal ownership and was occupied by Robert Thomas with his wife and grandson. Aged sixty-five and born in the village, Thomas earned his living as a 'haulier and carrier'.

Photographs from later years show some large families were brought up in the small buildings along the canal. Alfred Howse was lock-keeper at Latton Basin and lived in the cottage there with his wife Prudence. They also ran a small market garden business selling their produce in Cricklade market, taken either by boat or by donkey cart. In this view c.1915 they are surrounded by their ten children, including sons Joe and Frank and their eight daughters. (*Photo courtesy Edwin Cuss Collection*)

This wedding group photographed outside the roundhouse at Chalford on 6 March 1926 is of the Dowdeswell family. Great grandfather George (1829-1909) worked as a labourer, lock-keeper, toll-keeper and lengthman for the Canal Company, finally settling in the roundhouse in Chalford. In the Brimscombe Port attendance book, he is listed in the 1890s as still working the staff's twelve-day fortnight at the age of sixty-four. Grandfather Thomas (1872-1955) was a boatman and lock-keeper on the canal for his working life; one of his nine children was born at Puck Mill. Father Reginald (1899-1980) is seen surrounded by his family at his marriage; he was working on canal boats in 1925 and then moved into the canal cottage at Brimscombe Port, leaving the company's employ. When the County Council made an internal reorganisation of its continuing management of the canal (for water supply and control purposes), responsibilities were passed from its old Canal Committee to the Highways Committee. So the surviving staff moved from canal to road responsibilities, including Reginald who remained at work at Brimscombe, with responsibilities for water levels, until his retirement. He lived with his family first at Canal Cottage and then next door in Wharf House from 1948. Daughter Doreen was born in Canal Cottage. Both properties were demolished in the mid-1980s.

(Photo courtesy Doreen Phelps, Cricklade)

Further Reading

Not surprisingly for such a high profile enterprise, there is a considerable literature on the Thames & Severn Canal, with original records, archives and other primary material housed in the Gloucestershire Record Office. Catalogue lists are available to assist in studying this vast collection, and intended readers are well advised to be selective, if only to preserve a sense of balance when faced with such a formidable amount of material.

This section attempts to show the more significant and accessible secondary material, and follows the same sequence as this book, as a way of directing interest to certain subjects or sections of the canal. In every case, bibliographies given in these publications will direct the reader to further sources. Not all listed items remain in print.

General Canal History

The works of Charles Hadfield are central to any appreciation of the history of canals in Britain. *British Canals: An Illustrated History* is the core study, first published in 1950 with numerous editions since. The latest version is *Hadfield's British Canals,* edited by Joseph Boughey (Sutton Publishing 1998). The regional *Canals of the British Isles* series includes all the major studies of individual canals (including Household, see below), all published by David & Charles.

The Anatomy of Canals: The Early Years (1750-1800) and *The Mania Years (1800-1825),* by Anthony Burton & Derek Pratt, Tempus Publishing, 2001, 176pp and 2002, 176pp respectively.

Stroudwater Canal

The Stroudwater Canal, vol.I 1729-63 by Michael Handford, Moonraker Press, 1976, 93pp.

The Stroudwater Canal by Michael Handford, Alan Sutton Publishing 1979, 338pp.

Thames & Severn Canal

Humphrey Household's work is highly regarded and represents the expression of many decades of research. His principal publications include:

'Early Engineering on the Thames and Severn Canal', read at a meeting of the Newcomen Society on 11 January 1950 and published in *Engineering*, 27 January and 3 February 1950, and *Transactions* of the Newcomen Society, vol. 28 for 1951-3.

The Thames and Severn: birth and death of a canal. The author's MA thesis at the University of Bristol, 1957-1958.

'The Thames and Severn Canal' in *Journal of Transport History*, vol. viii, no.3, 1966, pp.129-40.

The Thames & Severn Canal, David & Charles 1969, new edition Alan Sutton Publishing 1983, 258pp.

Other general studies

The Thames and Severn Canal by J. Graham Espley and W.E. Duncan Young, Gazebo Books, Corsham 1969, 46pp.

The Thames & Severn Canal: a survey from historical photographs by David Viner, Hendon Publishing 1975, 44pp.

Stroudwater & Thames and Severn Canals Towpath Guide by Michael Handford & David Viner, Alan Sutton Publishing, 1984, reprinted 1988, 224pp.

The Stroudwater and Thames & Severn Canals in old photographs by Edwin Cuss and Stanley Gardiner, 1988, and *A Second Selection*, 1993, Alan Sutton Publishing, 160pp. respectively.

Chapter 2 Building and Running the 'Great Undertaking'

A Brief History of the Thames and Severn Canal by E.T. Gardom, Clerk to Gloucestershire County Council, January 1902, 50pp.

'Roundhouse' by Christopher Powell, *Waterways World*, October 1974, pp.20-1 (on the Thames & Severn Canal group)

'Roundhouses' by Patrick Thorn, *Waterways World*, January 1988, pp.58-9. (includes Thames & Severn and Staffs & Worcs. Canals)

Chapter 3 Leisure & Pleasure

The Flower of Gloster by E. Temple Thurston, first edition 1911, new edition with Forward by L.T.C. Rolt, David & Charles 1968; new edition with commentary by David Viner, Alan Sutton Publishing 1984, 146pp.

My Holidays on Inland Waterways by Peter Bonthron, first edition 1916, second edition 1917.

Saul Adam by John Poole, Thornhill Press, Gloucester 1973.

Chapter 4 Restoration

The Cotswold Canals Trust publishes *The Trow* quarterly for its members; this has become the best archive of restoration activity since the first Trust was formed in 1972. In addition, the Trust publishes three very useful booklets *A Guide to the Cotswold Canals*, and *Around the Cotswold Canals : Ten Circular Walks*, vols. One and Two. Full details from Trust office at 44 Black Jack Street Cirencester GL7 2AA (phone 01285 643440). A most attractive full-colour Towpath Map (with superb photography) published in 2001 by Stroud District Council jointly with the Trust and other bodies covers the route up to Daneway and Sapperton.

'Restoration Report : Stroudwater Navigation' by Keith Goss, *Waterways World*, June 1985, pp.62-4 (see also *Waterways World*, December 1979, pp.30-1).

'Let's do the easy bit first' by Martin Ludgate, *Waterways World*, July 2000, pp.44-8.

The Cotswold Canals Walk: Stroudwater, Thames & Severn by Gerry Stewart, Countryside Matters, 2000, 96pp.

To Maintain and Improve: the History of the Lower Avon Navigation Trust by D.H. Burlingham, Tempus Publishing, 2000, 160pp.

Restoring the Kennet & Avon Canal by Peter Lindley-Jones, Tempus Publishing, 2002, 208pp.

'The Cotswold Canals' by Derek Pratt, *Canal Boat and Inland Waterways*, March 2003, pp.62-7.

Chapters 5-7 Stroud to Brimscombe, Brimscombe Port into the Golden Valley and Climbing to Daneway

Severn Traders: the West Country Trows and Trowmen by Colin Green, Black Dwarf Publications, Lydney, 1999, 180pp. See also the same author's 'The Severn Trow', *Archive*, no.12, 1996, pp.3-20.

'Built at Brimscombe Port' by Wilf Rowles, *Waterways World*, March 1978, pp.52-7 (on the boat building yard of Clark and Abdela & Mitchell).

'Steamboat-Builders of Brimscombe' by A.M. Langford in Gloucestershire Society for Industrial Archaeology (GSIA) *Journal*, for 1987, pp.33-41 and 1988, pp.3-20.

Edwin Clark: Steamboat Builder of Brimscombe by Lionel Lacey-Johnson with Tony Langford, privately published, 2000, 62pp.

Chalford Place by Juliet Shipman, 1979, 16pp. (a history of the house – latterly the Company's Arms – and its clothier families).

'To Serve the Watermen' by Stroud Local History Society, *Gloucestershire History*, No. 5, 1991, pp.5-7 (a study of canalside pubs).

Chapter 8 Sapperton Tunnel

'Canal Tunnels' by Peter Roberts, *Waterways World*, May 1975, pp.24-7.

'On the threshold of darkness: canal tunnel restoration in Gloucestershire' by David Viner, *Country Life*, 18 January 1979, pp.162-3.

Village Heritage and *Village Camera* by Miss Pinnell and the children of Sapperton School, Alan Sutton Publishing 1986, 112pp and 1990, 124pp respectively.

Chapter 9 Along the summit to Cirencester

'Canal Pumping Engines' by Jim Andrew, *Industrial Archaeology Review*, vol. XV No.2 Spring 1993, pp.140-59.

Cirencester and the Thames & Severn Canal by David Viner, Corinium Museum, Cirencester Brief Guides, 1974, 6pp.

'The Thames & Severn Canal in Cirencester' by David Viner, in *Studies in the archaeology and history of Cirencester*, ed. A.D. McWhirr, BAR Oxford 1976, pp.126-4.

Chapter 10 & 11: Siddington to Cricklade Wharf and the Eastern section to the Thames

Memories of Home in a Cotswold Village by John A. Farmer, Cheltenham, nd but *c*.1924, 50pp. A remembrance of local characters and natural history in and around Upper Siddington and the canal wharf.

'Narrow Boats on the Thames' by David Blagrove, *Waterways Journal*, vol. 4, Spring 2002, pp.5-26.

For the study of buildings, see *Gloucestershire 1: The Cotswolds* in the Pevsner Buildings of England series, by David Verey and Alan Brooks, Penguin Books, revised third edition 1999, 828pp.

For the mills in particular, see *Gloucestershire Woollen Mills* by Jennifer Tann, David & Charles, 1967, 254pp and two books by Stephen Mills & Pierce Riemer: *The Mills of Gloucestershire*, Barracuda Books 1989, 160pp. and *Gloucestershire Mills in Camera*, Quotes Limited 1991, 80pp.

Footnote

Even in the few months since this book was first published, changes have occurred. What remained of the lengthsman's cottage at the Daneway entrance to Sapperton tunnel (p.96) has been flattened. More encouraging news is the acquisition by British Waterways of much of Brimscombe Port (Chap. 6) and the property of Inglesham (p.153) – roundhouse, warehouse, lock and bridge – so spearheading the restoration campaign. Plans are well advanced to construct a new Western Spine Road bridge (p.138) to improve access and to relieve this long-standing (and dangerous) barrier. Towpath improvements include the opening up of the short section at Siddington on the Cirencester arm beyond the site of Pools bridge and behind Pound Close (p.123). The restoration campaign for the Cotswold Canals continues to be fully reported in *The Trow* and the various waterways magazines.
May 2003

Index

Numbers in **bold** refer to illustrations.